GREAT WAR BRITAIN
LIVERPOOL
Remembering 1914-18

GREAT WAR BRITAIN

LIVERPOOL

Remembering 1914–18

PAMELA RUSSELL

The History Press

For my husband, David, my son, Christopher,
and my daughter-in-law, Sarah

Also for Janet and Graeme Arnot and Harold
and Vicky Russell

First published 2018

The History Press
The Mill, Brimscombe Port
Stroud, Gloucestershire, GL5 2QG
www.thehistorypress.co.uk

© Pamela Russell, 2018

The right of Pamela Russell to be identified as the Author
of this work has been asserted in accordance with the
Copyright, Designs and Patents Act 1988.

British Library Cataloguing in Publication Data.
A catalogue record for this book is available from the British Library.

ISBN 978 0 7509 7039 6

Typesetting and origination by The History Press
Printed in Great Britain

CONTENTS

TIMELINE

1914

28 June 1914

Assassination of Archduke Franz Ferdinand in Sarajevo

4 August 1914

Great Britain declares war on Germany

6 August 1914

Liverpool men killed when HMS Amphion hits a German mine

23 August 1914

Battle of Tannenberg commences

27 August 1914

Lord Derby calls for a Liverpool 'battalion of Pals'

31 August 1914

Recruitment begins: by 10 a.m. 1,000 men have enlisted

6 September 1914

First Battle of the Marne

19 October 1914

First Battle of Ypres

7 December 1914

First shell-shock patients admitted to Red Cross Military Hospital, Maghull

1915

25 April 1915

Allied landing at Gallipoli

7 May 1915

Lusitania sunk. Civilian passengers and many Liverpool crew members killed

24 May 1915

Grand Military Gymkhana at Knowsley Hall with artillery and cavalry displays

31 May 1915

First German Zeppelin raid on London

20 December 1915

Allies finish their evacuation of and withdrawal from Gallipoli

1916

24 January 1916

*The British government
introduces conscription*

21 February 1916

Battle of Verdun commences

31 May–1 June 1916

*Battle of Jutland: over 150 men and boys
posted as missing in* Liverpool Echo

4 June 1916

Brusilov Offensive commences

1 July 1916

*First day of the Battle of the Somme
with 57,000 British casualties*

27 August 1916

Italy declares war on Germany

18 December 1916

Battle of Verdun ends

1917

6 April 1917

*The United States declares
war on Germany*

9 April 1917

Battle of Arras

27 July 1917

*Wing of Knowsley Hall offers convalescence
to women munitions workers*

31 July 1917

Third Battle of Ypres (Passchendaele)

20 August 1917

Third Battle of Verdun

26 October 1917

Second Battle of Passchendaele

20 November 1917

Battle of Cambrai

27 November 1917

*Ewan Blackledge shot down by Lothar
von Richthofen, the Red Baron's brother*

7 December 1917

*The United States declares war
on Austria-Hungary*

1918

3 March 1918

Russia and the Central Powers sign the Treaty of Brest-Litovsk

21 March 1918

Second Battle of the Somme

15 July 1918

Second Battle of the Marne

8 August 1918

Battle of Amiens, first stage of the Hundred Days Offensive

22 September 1918

The Great Allied Balkan victory

27 September 1918

Storming of the Hindenburg Line

8 November 1918

Armistice negotiations commence

9 November 1918

Kaiser Wilhelm II abdicates, Germany is declared a republic

11 November 1918

End of war announced from the Town Hall balcony to cheering crowds

1919

5 August 1919

Afternoon tea celebration at the Derby estate: sports, games and naval rockets

ACKNOWLEDGEMENTS

The book honours and recognises all those people of Liverpool and the surrounding region who lived and served their country through the Great War.

Thank you to Nicola Guy, my editor at The History Press, with whom it continues to be a pleasure to work, and to David Stoker and Roger Hull of Liverpool Central Libraries for their co-operation, access to the city's splendid archive and permission to use extensive illustrative material.

Thanks to my husband, David Russell, whose technical and photographic expertise has made possible the illustrations in this book.

Other acknowledgements include: Bill Borland, Linda Brown, Les Hewitt, Bruce Hubbard, Andrew Latimer, Gillian Morgan, John K. Rowlands and Christopher Russell.

INTRODUCTION

It is an honour to be asked to write this book, the purpose of which is to tell the story of the people of Liverpool and the surrounding region, including the area from Southport and Ormskirk in the north to the Wirral peninsula on the other side of the River Mersey, in the Great War.

The book will primarily focus on life at home against the background of one of the world's most dreadful conflicts. It is intended to be interesting and accessible to anyone who wants to know more about Liverpool and more about the people of Liverpool in the Great War.

It is intended to highlight the contribution of all those people of Liverpool and the surrounding region who lived and served their country through the Great War, as well as those who did not return to their homes and to their families. I have tried to include actual examples of real people from every group in Liverpool society, with their stories illustrating the events that affected them and many others.

There were men who survived but whose lives were changed forever by this catastrophic war. As well as those who were injured, upon whom change was forced, there were others who experienced events that changed the course of their lives by choice. There were families who lost their breadwinner, who could be father, son, brother or husband. The rest of their lives and those of their children were affected by their hardships and lost opportunities caused by poverty. And the lives of women were changed by the war in ways that could not have been predicted. Even now, it is only just being recognised how far the beginnings of altered attitudes and different opportunities for women can be found in their response to the nation's needs a hundred years ago. People saw what women could achieve and women surprised themselves at times by their capabilities.

Children were affected by the war. Sometimes obviously, because their fathers, uncles, older brothers and cousins were grievously injured or killed; sometimes just because their fathers were absent for four long years during the formative period of their childhood and came home, greatly changed, to children who, in many cases, scarcely knew them. As well, children lived for years with their own fears and the drawn-out anxiety of the women in their families.

My aim is to bring to life these people, not so very different from us, their lives and attitudes and their responses to circum-stances no one could have imagined in a world which, although only a century ago, was very different from that in which we live today.

1

OUTBREAK OF WAR

In 1914, Liverpool was the confident and prosperous 'second city of the Empire' and, as such, vital to the war effort. How did this city rise to prominence and how did her people respond to the challenge of the most devastating of wars?

The Bank Holiday weekend on which war was declared was reported by the *Liverpool Echo* with headlines boldly proclaiming 'Holiday Rush', 'Crowds Apparently Heedless of Crisis' and 'Landing Stage Scenes' and an article that continued with the following description:

Animated scenes were witnessed on the Liverpool Landing-stage, which has been thronged throughout the day with huge crowds of visitors, undeterred by the crisis, on their annual holiday. So great is the rush to Manx-land for the great August festival, and it is estimated that when the last steamers leave the Mersey tonight something like 20,000 people will have departed from Liverpool en route for various Isle of Man holiday resorts.

Excellent arrangements were made by the Isle of Man Steam Packet Co. for disposing of the vast crowd. No fewer than twelve sailings were arranged to be taken by some of the most popular steamers in the company's fleet. There will also be three sailings about midnight tonight.

The steamers belonging to the Liverpool and North Wales Steam Packet Co. were also filled with passengers for Llandudno, Beaumaris, and the Menai Straits, while the traffic on the New Brighton ferry boats was considerably in excess of the normal.

Clearly, this is an area with plenty of people who are not easily shaken by external threat, determined to continue to enjoy the summer, and able to afford to enjoy their leisure. How will they respond to duty's call?

The contribution of the people of this region to the national effort in the Great War was enormous and tremendously varied because, as well as the huge numbers of men who joined the army, Liverpool is a maritime city and had many of its menfolk already at sea, in the Royal Navy or the Merchant Navy, when the war began. The surrounding area also had some of the best agricultural land in the country, so as well as feeding itself and feeding its towns and cities, this region of farms and market

Liverpool's May Day parade in Lime Street, 1914 – a lively scene.

gardens, sometimes known as 'the salad bowl of England', began to send food further afield.

The ancient West Derby Hundred, the most westerly region of the land that is described as 'inter Ripam et Mersham' (between the Ribble and the Mersey) in the Domesday Book of 1086, is a region that perceived Liverpool to be its major city and natural heart in 1914, as it does today. It was from the whole of this region that many of the men who enlisted in the King's (Liverpool) Regiment originated.

The geographical position of Liverpool on the River Mersey, facing westward, was crucial to the part it played in this war. But Liverpool's position had always been crucial to its fortunes; the growth of Liverpool from its origins as a small village over the centuries to the great city that it had become by the beginning of the twentieth century had come about because of its position.

In 1199, John became King of England as well as Lord of Ireland. In a charter of that year to Henry of Lancaster, John omitted Liverpool, which had previously been part of the Honour of Lancaster. John wanted Liverpool in his own hands, having recognised its position as a convenient port for Ireland. The 'pool' offered a safe harbour where men and supplies could take passage to and from Liverpool. In 1207, John made Liverpool a borough and a port by Letters Patent.

Liverpool began to prosper because of its ideal situation for trade. At this time, there was a transfer of population from West Derby, the capital manor of the Hundred, to Liverpool. This was one of the first occasions when Liverpool's development attracted an incoming energetic and forward-looking population. There were to be many more such times in Liverpool's history that would lead to the extraordinary diversity of the people, who, at the beginning of the Great War, were called Liverpudlians.

King John was seen as the patron of Liverpool's growing prosperity and importance, so his heraldic badge became that of Liverpool. The Liver Bird, recognised worldwide, is the Eagle of St John, holding, in its beak, a sprig of broom, or *Planta genista*, to give it its Latin name. The symbol of Liverpool, seen on its corporate seal, is the armorial badge of John Plantagenet.

One of the important features of Liverpool in the Great War was its position as a deep-sea port with extensive docks facing the United States. From the first dock of 1715, the Liverpool docks grew and expanded to the south and to the north along the river. During the eighteenth century, the number of ships using the port rose from 102 in 1700 to 4,746 in 1800.

From this time onward, the port and its trade were constantly growing and, eventually, the shoreline from Garston to Bootle had the greatest range of docks in the world, 7 miles of which was served by the overhead railway. This was the first overhead railway outside London and, in 1893, the first in the world to have automatic electric signalling.

At the end of the eighteenth century, Liverpool was an attractive and prosperous place. It has been said that there are more Georgian buildings, terraces and squares in Liverpool than exist in Bath. But overcrowding and neglect caused some of these beautiful buildings to be threatened with destruction by 1914. Fortunately, today, many have been conserved and restored.

Liverpool's population in 1700 was about 6,000; by 1800, it was nearly 80,000. By the beginning of the twentieth century, it was 684,958. This massive increase was begun by the Agricultural Revolution, through which the countryside was enabled to feed the towns and cities. And the increase was reinforced by the Industrial Revolution, which brought many people into the towns to seek work. Liverpool's population also grew because of immigration. Some people were drawn to Liverpool as a place of opportunity.

By 1813, one tenth of the population was from rural Wales. John Hughes, the first elected mayor of Liverpool, was a Welshman. The city was home to a large Welsh population and, because of this, and because the more prosperous Welsh people would travel to Liverpool to shop, it was sometimes referred to as the 'capital of North Wales'. Eisteddfods were held in Liverpool in 1884, 1900 and as late as 1929.

Other incomers were from Scotland, like my paternal ancestors who were crofters and fisherfolk from the west coast, who came in the booming years of the late eighteenth century, to fish off the north shore and sell their catch, initially from a market stall and, later, from fish shops, to a hungry and growing population. There were well-known Scots in shipping, including McAndrew, Elder and Laird. And people poured into Liverpool from other parts of England too. Some came from the neighbouring county of Cheshire, or from the rest of Lancashire. Some were from further afield, like my husband's great-grandfather, Charles Smith Russell, a corn merchant, who in the nineteenth century came from London to Liverpool, then 'the wheat barometer of the world'. In 1805, the first Corn Exchange was built. In 1847, the Corn Laws were abolished and Liverpool's corn trade grew even more rapidly; its warehouses were extended and, in 1853, an association of corn merchants, the Liverpool Corn Trade Association, was formed. By 1895, stocks of grain in Liverpool were greater than those in any European port.

As a port, Liverpool became home to people from all over the world. It had one of the earliest Chinese communities, but the actual numbers were not large. In 1911, the Chinese population of Liverpool numbered just 403, but this was probably the largest group in any city in the country.

There was also a black population, also from an early date, but there are discrepancies in recording their origin. West Africans, possibly as a result of the Elder Dempster shipping line's links with that region, West Indians, Lascars, Asians and African-Americans were all to be seen in the dockland area, and, although some settled in Liverpool, they were often, literally, a floating population and were gone with the tide.

The long-established Jewish community were generally accepted because of their middle-class lifestyle and aspirations and their contribution to civic life. There was also a comparatively large German presence in the city and this was to prove problematic in the wake of the sinking of the *Lusitania*. The Germans were to provide a focus for all the feelings of anger and distress, or opportunism, felt at that time.

The Irish potato famine in the middle of the 1840s had caused millions of Irish people to cross the Irish Sea to Liverpool. Many of them hoped to continue their journey to the

States or elsewhere. Moreover, many were diseased or starving and most had no means of support. Famine meant that almost half a million people entered Liverpool from Ireland, of whom over 100,000 did not remain in the city. But it still caused a huge increase in population; by 1851, the population of Liverpool was over 375,000, of whom approximately a quarter were Irish in origin, although by this time, there were many Liverpool-Irish children. These large numbers caused hardship and want for many, not just the new arrivals but the existing labouring classes, now obliged to compete for work. There were great problems concerning health and housing, which had by no means been entirely overcome by 1914.

However, many of the 'Liverpool firsts' that grew out of efforts to respond to poverty and squalor were later adopted by the whole nation. These included the appointment of a medical officer of health, a district nursing service, the first public wash-houses, schools for the blind and for the deaf and dumb, and a number of hospitals. By the beginning of the Great War, as a result of tackling various problems, there had been many improvements in healthcare and other social advances.

Liverpool was involved in almost every aspect of the trade and industry of the nation. There was a period when several Liverpool potteries, including the Herculaneum Pottery Works, rivalled that of Wedgwood. More memorable, because of the cultural benefits to the nation of the Tate fortune, was sugar refining (Tate was not joined by Lyle until 1921). Linked with this trade was sweet manufacture – Tavener Routledge, Williams and Barker & Dobson are all Liverpool firms. Brewing was another major industry in Liverpool, with Threlfalls and Walker's breweries among the best known. The founder of Walker's Brewery gave a generous sum toward the funding of the magnificent art gallery that bears his name. Tobacco was a huge Liverpool import. The first recorded import of tobacco, believed to be the first ever import from the United States, was in 1648. Involved in this trade were the landed gentry of the area, the Norrises of Speke Hall and the Blundells of Ince and Little Crosby. Tobacco imported through Liverpool was of such great volume that the

Stanley bonded warehouse was the largest in the world. Tobacco would prove to be an important factor in keeping up the morale of the troops, and appeals were made to the public to contribute to 'smokes' for the troops.

In commerce, too, Liverpool led the nation. Martins Bank began in 1593 in a tavern, at the Sign of the Grasshopper, which, along with the Liver Bird, became a part of its emblem. Martins Bank was subsumed by the present-day Barclays Bank. The Liverpool Underwriters' Association was formed in 1803; insurance companies, including the Royal Liver Friendly Society and the Liverpool Victoria Friendly Society, thrived.

As a direct consequence of the growth and prosperity of Liverpool, department stores flourished. Owen Owen and T.J. Hughes, both founded by Welshmen, were opened in the nineteenth century. Lewis's, founded by David Lewis, who came from Liverpool's Jewish community, opened during the same period; by the beginning of the twentieth century, this was probably the largest store in the north of England.

At the beginning of the Great War, Liverpool's Bold Street, where the expensive ladies' outfitters and dressmakers, Cripps, was situated, was still known as 'the Bond Street of the North'. There were also many smaller but equally exclusive shops, such as furriers, tailors and milliners, in this exclusive shopping street.

The city also offered work in the construction industry, in rail and road transport, in shipbuilding, in manufacturing pharmaceuticals, in engineering and manufacture and in commerce at various levels, from office boys, to clerks, supervisors and managers. High levels of employment meant that money was in circulation with benefits to the local economy.

Women were able to find work in factories, offices, schools, nursing, shops, dress-making and tailoring establishments, although many of these employed only single women. The largest employment for women in 1914 was still domestic service; there were plenty of opportunities for cooks, kitchen-maids, housemaids and parlourmaids in the houses of the wealthy manufacturers and merchants. And even a clerk, of whom there were many all over the city, would strive to maintain a standard of living that included the employment of a maidservant, or, at the very least, a daily cleaner for rough work such as scrubbing. 'Dailies' were often married women or widows, who undertook laundry work at home – 'took in washing' – in order to survive.

LIVERPOOL'S POPULATION
Liverpool's population was between 750,000 and 800,000 people during the Great War. Despite numerous office workers and clerks in the city's companies, many of the poorer city dwellers were on low and unreliable wages, with rent taking about a third of the week's income of the casual labouring class.

The Liverpool docks provided employment for many men, but the system of employing them was based on casual labour. Men were 'taken on' by the day, or more often by the half-day at the hiring stands along the dock road; they were paid accordingly and this method of payment allowed no possibility of planning family expenditure. Dockers' wives and others in the labouring classes were obliged to shop daily, unable to organise their purchases to the best advantage. This lifestyle was not conducive to the application of those skills in household management which were evident in the more stable strata of the working class, where every penny, through fore-thought and thrift, was stretched to do the work of two pence. Dockers needed to live near the docks in order to know where and when work was available, so there were communities in the dockland areas where most families were living a 'from hand to mouth' existence.

So Liverpool, with its imposing architecture, including St George's Hall, the Walker Art Gallery and the William Brown Library and Museum, today housing part of the World Museum Liverpool and Liverpool Central Library, was home to wealthy merchants and industrialists, a comfortable middle class and an artisan class for whom there was plentiful employment. But alongside this pride and prosperity, there was also poverty, felt by casual labourers and, most painfully, by families where there was no breadwinner at all, even one with an unreliable form of employment.

To add to the existing splendour of the city, in 1907 the Mersey Docks and Harbour Board opened its impressive premises, followed by the iconic Liver Building in 1911 and the

Cunard Building on which work began in 1914. At the beginning of the Great War, the Three Graces, as they are now called, were already a focal point on Liverpool's waterfront.

In 1914, Liverpool was the maritime heart of a great nation and Britain was a country whose power had increased worldwide for over a century. The British people were accustomed to their elevated status in the world and their belief in their right to govern and conquer was unshakeable.

But events were now in train that would change the lives of the people of Liverpool, the country and the world. These events meant that Liverpool would become the lifeline for the nation, with thousands of ships in hundreds of convoys sailing into and out of Liverpool to keep the country fed and to support the immense war effort. The weapons, food, fuel and troops coming through Liverpool made it possible for Britain to win the war.

On 28 June 1914, the Archduke Franz Ferdinand, heir to the Austrian throne, visited Sarajevo with his wife. A bomb was thrown at them but it missed. They continued their visit but were later shot and killed. To British politicians, this regrettable occurrence did not seem to be any different, initially, from other events in a notoriously unsettled part of the world.

LEEDS–LIVERPOOL CANAL

When war began, many young boatmen were allowed to join up or move into jobs in industry. By 1917, this loss of skill became a problem and a battalion of soldier boatmen were trained to work with older boatmen in the vital work of moving goods necessary for the war effort.

But the Austrians believed the assassin to be Serbian and on 23 July, Austria-Hungary, with the backing of Germany, delivered an ultimatum to Serbia, demanding among other things that they should be allowed to investigate the assassination themselves. Despite suggesting arbitration to settle the dispute, the Serbs begin to mobilise their troops. In response, Austria-Hungary severed diplomatic ties with Serbia and also began to mobilise.

The British foreign secretary, Sir Edward Grey, was concerned that if events were allowed to escalate, the Russians would intervene on Serbia's behalf and that Germany, allied to Austria-Hungary, would become involved on the opposite side. So Britain made efforts to organise a conference among the major European powers to resolve the dispute. France, Italy and Russia agreed to participate, but Germany declined.

Germany's role in the preliminaries of the Great War is complex. There is no doubt that the Kaiser himself was a militaristic figure with imperial ambitions, eaten up with envy of the British Empire and resentful of the fact that, although his mother was the oldest of the children of Queen Victoria, his Uncle Bertie, who became known as Edward VII, inherited Queen Victoria's throne and empire because he was her eldest son. The king in 1914 was George V, who had succeeded his father in 1910. Germany had been arming itself and building up its navy for years, waiting for an opportunity to advance its ambitions.

The arch-enemy: the Kaiser's demonic image.

Britain had no ambition in mainland Europe; its political interest there had been to keep a balance so that no threat grew up against the British Empire. Winston Churchill, who had been appointed to the Admiralty in October 1911, had been keeping Britain ahead of the Germans and strengthening the navy by expanding the number of dreadnoughts, the most powerful battleship of the time, in order to keep Germany in check.

On 28 July, the Austro-Hungarian Empire declared war on Serbia. The next day, Britain called for international mediation to resolve the worsening crisis. Russia urged German restraint, but also began to mobilise its troops as a precaution. The Germans also began to mobilise themselves.

Events then began to move quickly and, it seems now, inexorably, toward widespread conflict. On 30 July, Austrian warships bombarded the capital of Serbia, Belgrade. In reaction to this attack on Serbia, Russia began full mobilisation of its troops. On 1 August, Germany declared war on Russia and France;

Little Belgian Refugees', 10 October 1914, was intended to rouse sympathy.

—THE LIVERPOOL COURIER. SATURDAY. OCTOBER 10. 1914.—

LITTLE BELGIANS AT LIVERPOOL.

"COURIER" PHOTO.'

Seven little Belgian children who are now the guests of Miss Heap at Eaton House, West Derby. They attend school every day, and the elder ones are making good progress in English. The children are depicted modelling in clay in the school yard.

the German army demanded safe passage through Belgium as it moved to attack France. When this was refused, the German response was swift and merciless. Cities were burnt and many Belgian people, including women, the elderly and children, were brutally killed.

The king of the Belgians entreated Britain for 'diplomatic intervention'; Sir Edward Grey stated to the House of Commons that Britain had a duty to Belgium as a matter of honour. But it was also clear that in its own national interest, Britain must intervene. Britain sent an ultimatum to Germany to withdraw from Belgium. But Germany needed to cross Belgium in order to strike at France and, by now, was utterly deaf to reason and rejected the demand. The Belgian people fled from their homeland in their thousands. Britain was known to have offered refuge to those fleeing persecution in the past, and enormous numbers of Belgians poured rapidly into the country.

The *Liverpool Echo* reported on 1 September 1914 that, after a bombing raid on Antwerp, large numbers of Belgian refugees were entering Britain and that some of them had arrived in Liverpool. Over the next few months, refugees were accepted across Liverpool and the surrounding area, including Birkenhead, Southport, Crosby and the Wirral.

WOUNDED BELGIANS AT THE NORTHERN HOSPITAL.

Wounded Belgians at present under treatment at the David Lewis Northern Hospital, Liverpool, photographed with members of the surgical and nursing staff.

'Wounded Belgians at the Northern Hospital' brought home the reality of events abroad.

LIVERPOOL MERCHANTS' HOSPITAL

The Liverpool Merchants' Hospital was also known as Liverpool Merchants' Mobile Hospital or No. 6 Hospital British Red Cross. It was funded by the Liverpool Chamber of Commerce and staffed by volunteers from the city. The intention was to design a hospital which could be easily assembled, then dismantled and taken to where it was needed most.

The Chamber of Commerce set up a committee to monitor expenditure, oversee the administration and record admissions. Lord Derby was committee chairman and took a great personal interest in the project. He was keen that there should be a recreation hut and also that facilities, including meals, should be provided for family members who had travelled to France to be with their badly injured loved ones.

Some of the staff, including the matron, Miss Whitson, stayed with the hospital throughout the war. She had previously been the matron at the Brownlow Hill Workhouse. Miss Whitson was awarded the Royal Red Cross for her war service at the hospital.

In March 1915, Mary Chavasse, known as May, became a lady helper to the Voluntary Aid Detachment with the Liverpool Merchants' Mobile Hospital. Her twin sister, Marjorie, had volunteered at a convalescent hospital for soldiers in Worcestershire. The twins were sisters to Noel Chavasse. They lived to celebrate their hundredth birthday in 1986.

The writer C.S. Lewis was treated for wounds received at the Battle of Arras at the hospital in Etaples and featured it in his book, *Spirits in Bondage*.

In June 1918, the area around Etaples came under heavy bombardment and orders came to close the hospital. The Medical Committee asked permission to continue its work and this was agreed. The army took down and re-erected the hospital at Deauville, which had been the original intention. The staff were demobilised on 17 December 1918.

Various hostels were set up to house the Belgians. In Port Sunlight, over a hundred men, women and children were temporarily settled in Hulme Hall, which was used as a hostel until they could be re-housed, more permanently, in the Manchester area at the end of November. In Liverpool, the Belmont Grove Workhouse was used as temporary accommodation for 300 Belgians in October 1914. Some of the refugees had been sent on from London, which had been their point of arrival.

Appeals for assistance were appearing in the *Liverpool Echo* and *Liverpool Courier*, along with photographs of the suffering of the refugees. There was widespread outrage at the way these people had been treated by the Germans. The appeals highlighted a wide range of needs for people who had been forced to flee their homeland, in fear of their lives, with so few of their belongings. Clothes and accommodation were the most pressing concerns, but there was also a requirement for hospital beds for the sick or wounded and free schooling for the children.

British and Belgian wounded soldiers at Allerton Beeches. All in it together.

On 20 October 1914, the *Liverpool Daily Post and Mercury* carried an article stating that the National Vigilance League had been inundated with offers of hospitality for the Belgian refugees who had found themselves in exile in Liverpool.

6—THE LIVERPOOL COURIER. FRIDAY, OCTOBER 16, 1914.—6

BRITISH AND BELGIAN WOUNDED AT LIVERPOOL.

Five British and nine Belgian wounded soldiers now at the residence of Mr. A. A. Booth at Allerton Beeches.

Liverpool people began sewing clubs and entertainment for the refugees, and Belgian refugee funds were set up in Liverpool and Birkenhead.

There were widespread efforts to provide for the Belgians. In an attempt to give them back some self-respect and independence, exhibitions of Belgian lace work were held as a way for families to raise money to support themselves. There were fundraising activities, such as a Chocolate Week and various Flag Days. Many of the refugees were trained as cabinet makers and were skilled craftsmen. Birkenhead Trades Council provided them with materials so that they could make small items to sell. The proceeds went to the lady mayoress's Belgian refugee fund.

FLAG DAYS
Flag Days were created to raise funds within months of the beginning of the Great War. Flag sellers were assisted by members of the Boy Scouts and the Boys' Brigade. One of the worthwhile causes was to raise funds to help prisoners of war in Germany.

The *Liverpool Echo* reported that there had been hundreds of offers of accommodation or monetary contributions, both large and small, from the people of Liverpool and the region. In the urgent need to respond immediately to the desperate plight of enormous numbers of refugees, there was, at first, no central registration. Indeed, there was no such register until late in 1914. So it is impossible to know how many Belgians came to Liverpool, or to Britain, or to know how long they stayed.

The arrival of the Belgians was a portent of the utter chaos into which Europe was shortly to be thrown.

Midnight on 3 August came and the Germans continued to ignore the British ultimatum. Sir Edward Grey, who, as foreign secretary, had done all he could to avert war, looked out at the gaslit dusk of that evening and declared prophetically, 'The lamps are going out all over Europe. We shall not see them lit again in our lifetime.'

On 4 August, Great Britain declared war on Germany. The declaration was binding on all dominions within the British Empire including Canada, Australia, New Zealand, India and South Africa. On the same day, the United States declared its neutrality.

2

Preparations at Home

Britain had the biggest navy in the world but one of the smallest armies. Winston Churchill, First Lord of the Admiralty, who was still not yet 40 years old, and who was in political charge of this most powerful navy, sent a signal to all ships: 'Commence hostilities against Germany.'

The second largest mobilisation of men in Liverpool was for the Royal Navy. More than 12,000 Liverpool men signed up to fight the war at sea. As a consequence of these large numbers, there were men from Liverpool on every single battleship between 1914 and 1918.

Liverpool was 'the second city of the Empire'. By 1914, over 30 per cent of all Britain's imports and exports came through the port, so Liverpool became a lifeline to the nation for the duration of the war, with hundreds of convoys sailing into the city to enable the country to function and support the war effort in many of its aspects. It cannot be overstated how vital to the country the food, fuel, weapons and troops that came into Liverpool were in waging war, securing victory and helping to liberate and change the face of Europe. Therefore, it is fair to suggest that the efforts of those working in various civilian roles in the port were as vital as those of the fighting forces.

Liverpool is a maritime city, so inevitably, after Churchill's signal, Liverpool men were immediately involved in warfare at sea, as the Germans began laying mines on the evening of 4 August.

'The Navy Wants Men.' Many Liverpool men were already at sea.

'Join the Royal Marines.' There was always a call for more men.

Conflict came quickly on the high seas after the declaration of war. In fact, the first Liverpool servicemen to be killed in the war were not soldiers; they were sailors.

On 5 August, the scout cruiser HMS *Amphion* was warned by a British fishing trawler in the North Sea that a ship was acting suspiciously and jettisoning unidentified objects overboard. It turned out to be the German minelayer, the *Königin Luise*, a former passenger ferry, masquerading as a British railway steamer, having been painted in the brown, yellow and black colours of the Great Eastern Railway ferry service. The German ship was chased and sunk, and HMS *Amphion* picked up some survivors.

In the early hours of 6 August, she set course for Harwich. Sadly, she ran into the minefield laid by the *Königin Luise* the previous day. An intense fire broke out, and *Amphion* struck another mine and sank. Although some survivors were picked up by other British vessels, the resulting explosion and fire killed 150 of her crew, including 33-year-old Private Robert Burns from Walton, a member of the Royal Marine Light Infantry, and Able Seaman Raymond Davenport, 21, the son of Tom and Priscilla Davenport, from Sunlight Street, off Belmont Road.

Another crucial task undertaken by Merseyside's shipping lines and seafarers was the blockade of Germany. A cruiser squadron was instituted by the Admiralty, and was based in Liverpool; in it there was a huge majority of Merseyside shipping and crews. The 10th Cruiser Squadron, as it was known, was crucial in the planning and successful tactics of the Royal Navy in the Great War.

Just as Liverpool's seafarers were immediately drawn into the war, so Liverpool's ferries were called upon to play their part. Two Mersey ferries, the *Daffodil* and the *Iris*, took part in the Zeebrugge Raid, where they saw action at the Mole. The Zeebrugge Raid was an attempt to stop Germany using Zeebrugge as a submarine base. The action was successful and both ferries returned to service on the Mersey after the war. They both needed extensive refitting before they were fit to continue their peacetime activities. When they returned to the Mersey in 1919, they were greeted with acclaim and 'Royal' status was granted to both ferries, *Iris* and

MERSEY FERRIES
On 23 April 1918, a successful battle involving former commercial vessels took place when two Mersey ferries, the *Daffodil* and the *Iris*, participated in the Zeebrugge Raid. The action was intended to stop Germany using Zeebrugge as a submarine base. Both ferries returned to service on the Mersey after the war.

Daffodil, in recognition of their gallant service to their country.

As well as the Mersey ferries, other commercial vessels, such as passenger liners and trawlers, were converted into war-worthy ships. This remarkable process was done in Liverpool and was considered a huge achievement. During the course of the war and especially at the beginning, seventeen liners were requisitioned by the Royal Navy and turned into armed merchant cruisers by skilled carpenters and engineers. One of the Laird-built ships, the *King Orry*, was converted into an armed boarding sloop. At the end of the

Wallasey Corporation Ferries.

H.M.S. IRIS II. & DAFFODIL IV.

Souvenir of Zeebrugge Raid

St. George's Day, 23rd April, 1918.
RETURNED TO MERSEY, 17th MAY, 1918.

PRICE - - - THREEPENCE.

Proceeds in Aid of Dependents of Zeebrugge Victims, Wallasey Red Cross and Soldiers' Funds.

LIVERPOOL:
CHARLES BIRCHALL, LTD., 17, JAMES STREET.

Souvenir of Zeebrugge Raid: local pride in the Royal Iris *and the* Royal Daffodil.

war, the *King Orry* led the surrendered German fleet into Scapa Flow. The liner *Campania* and the Isle of Man Steam Packet Company ferry *Ben Ma Chree* were converted on Merseyside into the first seaplane carriers.

Ships belonging to the numerous Liverpool shipping lines were involved in the war at sea and many suffered huge losses in ships and men. The Ellerman line, for instance, suffered heavy losses. A large proportion of its fleet was requisitioned by the government on the outbreak of war for conversion into armed merchant cruisers to increase the resources of the Royal Navy and for use as troop ships or munitions carriers. In all, 103 ocean vessels, with a total cargo capacity of 600,000 to 750,000 tons, were destroyed. The *City of Winchester* was the first merchant vessel to be destroyed in the war, in 1914. Another liner belonging to the Ellerman fleets was mined far from Europe. The *City of Exeter*, which had been a well-appointed passenger ship, struck a mine in the Indian Ocean.

Another Liverpool shipping line that was significantly involved in the war was Cunard. One of its commercial vessels, the liner *Carmania*, engaged a German enemy cruiser in battle in September 1914. The *Carmania* had been converted into an armed merchant cruiser, equipped with eight 4.7in guns. She was under the command of Captain Noel Grant and sailed from Liverpool to Shell Bay in Bermuda, where she subsequently engaged and sank the German merchant cruiser SMS *Cap Trafalgar*, during the Battle of Trindade. At the time *Cap Trafalgar*'s appearance had been altered to resemble *Carmania*.

Carmania suffered extensive damage and casualties among her crew. But, after repairs in Gibraltar, she patrolled the coast of Portugal and the Atlantic islands for the next two years. In 1916, she was summoned to assist in the Gallipoli campaign. From May 1916, she was used as a troop ship. After the war, the *Carmania* was used to transport Canadian troops back home.

CONVERSION OF COMMERCIAL VESSELS
Liverpool was at the forefront of converting commercial vessels, like trawlers, into warships. This difficult process was considered a remarkable achievement. During the war, seventeen liners were requisitioned by the Royal Navy and transformed into armed merchant cruisers by Liverpool's skilled engineers and other tradesmen.

The Cunard liner *Mauretania* held the Blue Riband from 1909 to 1929. This is an unofficial accolade given to the passenger liner crossing the Atlantic Ocean westbound in regular service with the record highest speed. A ship is not worthy of the Blue Riband unless the record speed is achieved following the westbound route against the Gulf Stream. The sinking of her sister ship, the *Lusitania*, in 1915 was to be one of the causes of the entry, the United States into the war.

During the period from 5 August 1914, the day following the British declaration of war, to the armistice of 11 November 1918, a total of 2,479 British merchant vessels and 675 British fishing vessels were lost as a result of enemy action, with respectively 14,287 and 434 lives lost. The Mercantile Marine War Medal was instituted by the Board of Trade and approved by the king to reward the war service of the officers and men of the Mercantile Marine who, while only trained as peacetime mariners, continued to serve while running the risk of being attacked at sea during the war.

The Mercantile Marine memorial on Tower Hill was designed by Sir Edwin Lutyens and commemorates the loss of 12,210 men. It was intended that the king, George V, would perform the unveiling ceremony, but as he was seriously ill, Queen Mary took his place, the first time she had played such a central role. The dedication on the memorial reads, 'To the glory of God and to the honour of twelve thousand of the Merchant Navy and Fishing Fleets who have no grave but the sea 1914–1918.'

My grandfather, Albert Sendall, was one of those who survived the awful experience of being torpedoed. This happened twice in thirty-six hours, when the ship that had rescued men from the water after the first incident was, in her turn, torpedoed and sank.

On 5 August 1914, Field-Marshal Lord Kitchener accepted the post of Secretary of State for War. He was a national hero of the Sudan and South African campaigns and, therefore, likely to appeal to the public as a military leader and figurehead.

Just over a decade earlier, the Boer War had been seen as a war to preserve the Empire. However, the British people also saw the eventual outcome of the conflict as confirmation of their supreme status in the world. The celebrations of the Relief

Postcard showing Lord Kitchener, minister of war: a national hero.

of Mafeking on 18 May 1900, and the instant promotion of Robert Baden Powell to the status of national hero, suggest that, although there had been a period of anxiety, the British public's belief in themselves and their invincibility had been re-established. The Boer War had also been a turning point in the use of propaganda, both by the British government and press and also by the Boer opposition.

Lord Kitchener was preparing for a long-drawn-out fight, not sharing the popular view that the war would be over by Christmas. There is little doubt that, at this stage, many of those who held the latter opinion were in a position to be better informed than the general populace, who were well accustomed to being victorious on all fronts.

In fact, Kitchener was one of the few leading soldiers or statesmen to predict a long and costly war and to foresee that the existing British Expeditionary Force (BEF) of six infantry divisions and four cavalry brigades would be far too small to play an influential part in a major European conflict. Later, when Lord Derby suggested that men should enlist for 'three years or for the duration', many people were astonished at his pessimism, which, in fact, was a realistic grasp on the situation.

The situation was complex. Britain was bound by treaty to assist Belgium, and the will to support this oppressed nation was also strong. Having declared war against Germany on 4 August, however, the country was resolute but unprepared.

The professional army was badly equipped and ridiculously small in comparison to the huge armies on the Continent. Britain's strength and defence was the Royal Navy. Her army comprised 450,000 men. This number included fewer than a thousand trained staff officers, and more than half of the rest were reservists. Kitchener warned the government that the war would be decided by the last million men that Britain could throw into battle. This meant that the army needed to be increased hugely in numbers of men and officers.

Robert Baden-Powell (B-P) now made a call that was intended to release men for the army. He had witnessed the useful part that the young boys of the Mafeking Cadet Corps had played during the Siege of Mafeking and believed that they had a vital role to play in a country at war.

Baden-Powell had established the Boy Scout movement on 24 January 1908. Now, he called on the Scouts to 'do their bit'. Immediately, in South Lancashire, many young boys who were Scouts volunteered and could be found helping the war effort in a variety of ways: in recruitment offices assisting with routine office tasks, distributing leaflets and acting as messengers. Scouts were also used to guard railway lines and stations, canals, telegraph and telephone lines, reservoirs and anywhere else that was seen as strategically important. Sea Scouts were used for coastal watching, and a proficiency badge could be earned for this service. As the war progressed, other proficiency badges that had relevance to the skills that were needed, such as first aid, meant that Scouts were able to help in hospitals and convalescent homes, and as food supplies were threatened, Scouts could earn their farming badge by working on the land in all weathers and by helping with the harvest of vital crops. Scouts were also fundraising across the country and raised enough money for five ambulances to be sent to the front.

The Girl Guides had only been established in 1910, under the leadership of Agnes Baden-Powell, B-P's sister, with his encouragement. Girls had clamoured to be allowed to join in with some of the excitement that they saw their brothers enjoying. War brought their chance to prove themselves and they rose to the challenge. Guides provided assistance in government offices, hostels, dressing stations and munitions factories. They packaged clothing to send to the men at the front; they were prepared to offer first aid after air raids and, all over the country, they tended allotments to help combat the food shortages. Like the Boy Scouts, their efforts released adults to serve the war effort. There was a pressing need for men to volunteer in numbers.

Conscription was, at this stage, politically unacceptable, so Kitchener decided to raise a new army of volunteers. On 6 August, Parliament sanctioned an increase in army strength of 500,000 men, and within days Kitchener had issued his first call to arms. This was for 100,000 volunteers, aged between 19 and 30, at least 1.6m (5ft 3in) tall and with a chest size greater than 86cm (34in).

Public belief in the invincibility of the British combined with a traditional desire to defend the underdog – in this case, Belgium. The male population was, on the whole, optimistic about victory and ready for the conflict. As well as issuing his first appeal for volunteers, Kitchener also allowed the part-time Territorial Force, which had been intended primarily for home defence, to expand and to volunteer for active service.

The King's (Liverpool) Regiment comprised more than thirty battalions. Their central base was at Seaforth Barracks but they were scattered variously about the city and the area. Now they raised another battalion. Within a fortnight of Kitchener's appeal, the War Office had given permission for Liverpool to raise K battalion of the King's (Liverpool) Regiment.

MERCHANT TAYLORS' SCHOOL

Merchant Taylors' School Cadet Force was recognised on 30 March 1915 and affiliated to the 6th (Rifle) Battalion King's (Liverpool) Regiment. Sixty-three of the 731 boys who served in the Great War joined what became known as 'the school's battalion'.

Cheery and very youthful bandsmen of the King's (Liverpool) Regiment.

EXPRESS. LIVERPOOL, TUESDAY, NOVEMBER 3, 1914.—3

COMRADES MARCH OUT.

"EXPRESS" PHOTO.

The Comrades of the 1st City Battalion of the King's (Liverpool) Regiment marched from Prescot, to-day, to Sefton Park for lunch, and afterwards through the streets of the city. Our photo shows the battalion being received at Sefton Park by Lord Derby.

1st City Battalion (KLR) received at Sefton Park by Lord Derby.

The *Liverpool Echo* reported that large crowds gathered in Lime Street, Liverpool, near the great railway station, to greet the return from their annual training camps of the Territorials of the numerous battalions of the King's (Liverpool) Regiment. The 1st King's was at Aldershot when mobilisation began and reinforcements were sent from Liverpool to bring the battalion up to strength. The *Echo* also described emotional parting scenes at Lime Street station when they left.

At this point, a crucial suggestion came from General Henry Rawlinson, who believed that men would be more willing to join the army if they knew that they could serve with people they already knew. So the call to arms was augmented by the decision to form such units, which came to be known as 'Pals battalions'. This seemed like a good idea and it certainly achieved its purpose. Young men enlisted together, trained together, went to the front together and faced the enemy together. These Pals battalions were formed by brothers, cousins, friends and workmates, boys who played football or other sports together and attended church together. So when they were ultimately killed together in horrifically large numbers, whole streets, villages, churches, clubs, towns and cities were faced with the impact of the loss of a generation. About 2,800 Liverpool Pals had been killed by the end of the war.

Edward George Villiers Stanley, the 17th Earl of Derby, was a patriot who expected a similar sentiment to motivate the men of Liverpool. An energetic man and a natural leader, Lord Derby was a former Grenadier Guard and Conservative MP. He was president of the city's Chamber of Commerce and chancellor of the University of Liverpool, and had served as Liverpool's lord mayor in 1911.

So when Lord Kitchener made an appeal for the first 100,000 volunteers in August 1914, Lord Derby moved quickly to ensure the city was at the forefront of the First World War recruitment drive and to test the idea of the Pals battalions.

He believed that there were many men, such as clerks and others engaged in commercial business, who would be willing to enlist in a battalion of Lord Kitchener's new army if they felt assured they would be able to serve with their friends and not be put in a battalion with unknown men as their companions.

The Right Honourable the 17th Earl of Derby: an inspirational leader.

THE RIGHT HON. THE EARL OF DERBY,
G.C.V.O., C.B.
LORD MAYOR OF LIVERPOOL.

Photo by Medrington's, Ltd., Bold Street, Liverpool.

LORD DERBY'S SONS (1)

Lord Derby's sons served during the First World War. Edward Montagu Cavendish Stanley was the eldest son of the 17th Earl. He was a captain in the Grenadier Guards, rising to brigade major by the end of the war, and decorated with a Military Cross the following year.

On 24 August, Lord Derby met with Kitchener to ask if he could raise a battalion from the city's commercial class. Three days later, he called in the Liverpool newspapers for local men to serve in a battalion of comrades. In fact, it was Lord Derby who first used the term 'Pals battalions'. He said that those enlisting would form 'a battalion of pals, a battalion in which friends from the same office fight shoulder to shoulder for the honour of Britain and the credit of Liverpool'.

Lord Derby's sons also served during the war. Later, Edward Stanley was elected Member of Parliament for Liverpool Abercromby in a by-election in 1917, but he left Parliament after

LORD DERBY'S SONS (2)
Oliver Frederick George Stanley, the second son of the 17th Earl, was commissioned into the Lancashire Hussars, attached to the Royal Artillery, and reached the rank of major. He was decorated with the Military Cross and awarded the Croix de Guerre. Later, as MP for Westmoreland, he held several ministerial posts.

THE CHRISTMAS BOX.
" And millions more like me, Kaiser !"
FROM "THE PASSING SHOW."

DEC 22 1915 p3

A Christmas gift from Lord Derby.

3.—EVENING EXPRESS, LIVERPOOL, MONDAY, SEPTEMBER 7,

LIVERPOOL COMRADES.

("EXPRESS" PHOTO.) Liverpool Comrades marching to St. George's Hall, headed by Major Ferdina nd Charles Stanley, D.S.O. (on left of photo.)

Liverpool Comrades march to St George's Hall led by Charles Stanley DSO.

the seat was abolished for the general election of 1918. He returned to Parliament in 1922, later becoming deputy chairman of the Conservative Party and serving in the Cabinet during the 1930s until his death in 1938. Edward Stanley became a brigade major and remained in the army until 1920. He was awarded the Military Cross in 1919 for his service in Italy.

Lord Derby was not to be disappointed in his appeal for volunteers. Despite the maritime nature of the port city of Liverpool, its men were far from slow in enlisting in the army.

On Monday, 31 August, recruitment began at St George's Hall in the centre of Liverpool. The large employers in the city had their own separate desks where men could enlist, and these included the major shipping companies, such as the White Star and Cunard lines, and other important trades in the city, including the Cotton Association, Corn Trade Association and the sugar and tobacco companies.

Queues of men formed rapidly, and by 10 a.m. 1,000 men had signed up – enough to fill the battalion Lord Derby had promised Lord Kitchener – but many more men were still waiting. Within five days the total had reached 3,000, and by October there were enough from the city and its environs to form four Pals battalions in the King's Liverpool Regiment.

On 18 August, the *Liverpool Daily Post and Mercury* stated that 'every effort was being made to be able to report that Liverpool was the first to place a new eight hundred strong battalion in the field'. Indeed, it is acknowledged that the city of Liverpool had one of the most successful and earliest recruitment campaigns. Liverpool's immediate response to Lord Derby's call to arms was so esteemed that King George V gave permission for the Pals to wear the Derby crest as their insignia. Lord Derby then proceeded to provide silver cap

TERRITORIALS
7th KING'S
JOIN
THE NEW
LOCAL COMPANIES
RECRUITING OFFICES OPEN IN
Stanley Road, Bootle
AND AT
WATERLOO AND SOUTHPORT.
HEADQUARTERS:-99 PARK STREET, BOOTLE

The 7th King's: local recruiting achievement.

badges for each of the men. Some of these were later given to wives, girlfriends, sisters or mothers to be worn as brooches, and some still survive in the families of Liverpool Pals. Lord Derby's war effort continued after the battalions formed; custom-built barracks large enough to house three Liverpool battalions were built on his estate at Knowsley.

Liverpool's success prompted other towns and cities to follow suit. Civic pride prompted cities to compete with each other to attract the greatest possible number of new recruits in the shortest time – this was one of the reasons for the success of the Pals recruitment. Local pride also meant that companies and firms vied with each other to have the highest recruitment figures; and personal pride meant that men from offices and other forms of employment did not want to be the ones who hung back while their colleagues enlisted.

There was another motivation to enlist that did not affect the office workers at whom Lord Derby's campaign had been initially directed. For many men in Liverpool and in other industrial towns, the army promised an escape from the poverty of everyday life.

'Step Into Your Place': civilians become soldiers.

'Enlist Now': defend the idyllic English countryside.

The army must have offered the opportunity to escape from low-paid or uncertain employment or from unemployment. Industrial areas and mining districts provided a disproportionate number of recruits per head of male population. In country areas, the wages for farm labourers were very low and opportunities for advancement were few. Army life meant regular pay – a shilling a day for privates – and also proper food, plain but substantial, and clothing which was superior to their well-worn garments. Army barracks also compared favourably with the living conditions experienced by many at the time.

It is clear that the army and the establishment were eager to recruit – indeed, it was essential that they did so in large numbers – yet the fact that many volunteers were rejected on medical grounds, suffering from the cumulative effects of poor diet, medicine and housing, supports the theory that the conditions of life for the lower working classes were producing pitiably poor physical specimens. The basic requirement of 5ft 3in in height with a chest measurement of over 34in seems very low a century later. Bantam battalions were formed from small, tough men, full of character, often from the deprived areas of cities like Liverpool and Glasgow. These battalions soon gained a reputation as brave, fierce fighters.

Recruitment standard lowered: many of the working class were not well grown.

Attempts to remedy the basic poor physique and, even, actual malnourishment of some of the new recruits required time, which was something that was in short supply. There was criticism of the pre-war government's defence policy, which had left the country's army at a disadvantage. There was also a realisation that the condition of the lower working classes was a matter that would have to be addressed. Despite the overwhelming response, there was a huge poster campaign to get people to join up, and the government still found it necessary to introduce conscription in 1916.

On 8 August 1914, the Defence of the Realm Act (DORA) was passed. The government granted itself wide-ranging powers for the duration of the war; these included the right to requisition buildings or land needed for the war effort.

When it was introduced, DORA was a comparatively simple Act, passed in order to control communications and the nation's ports, and to subject civilians to the rule of military courts, when necessary. Another form of control was implemented when the trade unions began to work with the government to prevent strikes.

The Act was amended six times during the course of the war and one of the key amendments permitted the government to seize factories and land in order to produce the enormous amount of munitions and weapons that were needed to wage war. Under the Defence of the Realm Act the government was empowered to take over the coal mines, the railways and shipping.

This led directly to the need for women to enter the workforce in large numbers and to the concentration of workers in urban areas. This upheaval led to irreversible political, demographic and social changes which continue in the twenty-first century, including the introduction of British Summer Time and the widening of police powers.

Regulations were introduced that made apparently innocuous activities into criminal offences. Such peacetime activities as flying kites, starting bonfires, buying binoculars and feeding bread to wild birds were now outlawed. There were reasons for all these restrictions. Flying a kite or lighting a bonfire might attract Zeppelins and feeding bread to birds was a waste of food.

DEFENCE OF THE REALM ACT (DORA), AUGUST 1914

The first Defence of the Realm Act went through Parliament on 8 August 1914. It took only four days to receive the royal assent and was gazetted on 11 August 1914. This was extremely rapid, but its provisions were seen by all parties as vital to the security of the nation and to increase productivity.

Potential problems were the trade unions, the suffragettes and 'spies in our midst'. Some clauses were clearly necessary to protect information: no one was allowed to spread rumours about military matters or to talk about military or naval matters in public places. Some aspects of DORA related to possible spying or attempts at sabotage: no one was allowed to buy binoculars or trespass on railway lines or bridges; no one was allowed to use invisible ink when writing abroad.

Some aspects related to civil order and morals: the government could censor newspapers; beer was watered down, no one could buy a round of drinks in pubs and opening hours were cut. Whisky and brandy could not be purchased in railway refreshment rooms.

The government could take over any factory or workshop or any land that it deemed necessary. British Summer Time was introduced, which was intended to increase production.

Some of the other provisions may need a little explanation. Lighting bonfires, setting off fireworks and flying a kite could attract Zeppelins. The ban on feeding bread to horses or chickens was part of the drive to conserve food – this prohibition was introduced after the beginning of food rationing.

Those who offended against the provisions of DORA were dealt with by military courts and over a million people were prosecuted. Most of them received short prison sentences or were fined. Eleven people were found guilty of spying and executed.

At first, people were surprised and resentful. But particularly after rationing was introduced in 1917, the Act was better understood, taken seriously, and obeyed less grudgingly.

Also unpopular were the restrictions on alcohol. Alcoholic drinks were watered down and public house opening times were restricted to from noon to 3 p.m., and from 6.30 p.m. to 9.30 p.m. This requirement for a gap in public drinking hours remained in place until 1988, when a new Licensing Act was introduced.

Another form of social control introduced by DORA was censorship: 'No person shall by word of mouth or in writing spread reports likely to cause disaffection or alarm among any of His Majesty's forces or among the civilian population.' This was received with understanding by the general public, although it was frustrating to receive letters that were so heavily censored that they told the recipient very little about what was happening to their husbands and sons.

There was to be no discussion of naval or military matters, which seems eminently reasonable. The law was obviously meant to help prevent invasion and to keep morale at home high. It included censorship of journalism and of letters coming home from the front line. The press was subject to controls on reporting troop movements, numbers or any other operational information that could be exploited by the enemy. People who breached the regulations with intent to assist the enemy could be sentenced to death.

3

WORK OF WAR

The overwhelming response by men to the call to arms meant that there was a pressing need to replace the volunteers who had gone to the front by employing women in the jobs they had left behind. Inevitably, these large numbers of recruits had left gaps in the workforce and, later in the war, conscription made this need even more urgent.

There had been women in the workforce before the war, but these were mainly in textiles, particularly in dress-making, as sewing machinists and milliners. In Lancashire, many women,

'Boys Come Over Here': many men had pals who had already enlisted.

Female road sweepers in Liverpool, March 1916.

TICKETS, PLEASE!

EXPRESS PHOTO.
One of the women ticket collectors now on duty at Lime-street Station. She wears a navy-blue costume with black buttons, with the words "Ticket Collector" on her hat. In her hand is the usual punching instrument.

EVENING EXPRESS MAY 20 1915

A woman ticket collector at Lime Street station, 1915.

including married women, worked in the mills. But the war meant that women now entered the workforce in huge numbers, doing jobs that had previously been exclusively performed by men. Indeed, women now began to undertake tasks which they had previously been thought physically incapable of doing.

Between 1914 and 1918, more than 1,600,000 women were employed, primarily as land workers and in factories, especially in the dangerous munitions factories, which were employing 950,000 women by the end of the war. But they also found employment in government departments, public transport and the Post Office, as police officers, as clerks in business and in childcare.

Women's expectations about the type of work that they might successfully undertake changed. Many women left service, never to return, because the independence of their new life-style discouraged them from returning to a world 'below stairs' where their employer could dictate how their sparse leisure time could be spent, which church they attended and whether they could have boyfriends or marry. They also discovered that they could earn more money in a factory than they had ever had as a maidservant.

Ladies Company of Signallers in the Liverpool Home Defence Corps, 1915.

LIVERPOOL ECHO.

MAY 18 1915

SIGNALLERS IN HOME DEFENCE CORPS

" Echo " photograph of a signalling section (under Miss Radcliffe) of the Ladies' Company (over 100 strong) of the Liverpool Home Defence Corps, which drills each Sunday morning in the schoolyard, Boaler-street.

Home Service Corps Review, *1917.*

Inevitably, this had consequences for the families who had employed them. Pupils of Merchant Taylors' School for Girls in Crosby, most of whom were fee-paying, found that household duties took up part of the time that had been previously available for homework. Nevertheless, the headmistress, Miss Shackleton, believed that if girls were to undertake new tasks, they should learn how to do them well, and in 1915 domestic studies were extended to include cookery and laundry work. Girls were also encouraged to use the holidays to undertake some practical work.

At first, the entry of women into the workforce was greeted with hostility, partly because of genuine and sincere doubts about whether women could carry out some of the more physically demanding tasks. But male workers, seeing

MIDDLE-CLASS CHANGES
During the summer holidays of 1915, thirty-seven Merchant Taylors' girls learned to cook; fifty became more skilled at housework, while twenty-seven were able to sew and darn. Girls were also advised by their headmistress that they should learn to mend their own bicycles.

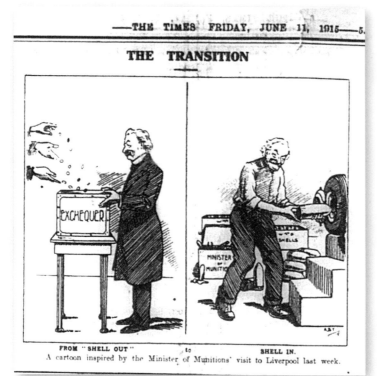

—THE TIMES FRIDAY, JUNE 11, 1915—5.

THE TRANSITION

EXCHEQUER

MINISTER of MUNITIONS

SHELLS

FROM "SHELL OUT" to SHELL IN.
A cartoon inspired by the Minister of Munitions' visit to Liverpool last week.

Lloyd George visits Liverpool: later a charismatic prime minister.

Huge numbers of munitions workers were women, serving in a dangerous occupation.

that women were willing to work for lower wages than they had been paid, worried that there would be a general lowering of rates of pay after the war, or even that their jobs would be lost permanently to women.

Many skilled men had enlisted and women's willingness to learn could not entirely make up for their loss. However, a solution to this problem was known as dilution, a process whereby complex tasks were broken down into simpler activities that non-skilled women workers could accomplish.

Under the Defence of the Realm Act, David Lloyd George became the Minister of Munitions and set up state-run munitions factories. The Munitions of War Act 1915 meant that munitions factories had fallen under the sole control of the government.

Women's work in munitions factories is one of the best-known areas of female employment in the Great War. The task of so-called munitionettes was very dangerous, but comparatively

A typical bay in Lambeth Road shell factory.

NATIONAL SHELL FACTORY LAMBETH ROAD, LIVERPOOL.
MACHINE SHOP.

We're both needed to serve the Guns!

FILL UP THE RANKS!
PILE UP THE MUNITIONS!

'We're both needed to serve the Guns': a united front.

well paid, for, although the women only got half the men's wages, it was still more than most had received in their former jobs, so the motivation to do this highly necessary work was not only patriotic, but also governed by economic reasons.

Mary MacArthur, secretary since 1903 of the Women's Trade Union League, demanded that women should be paid as much as the men employed in the same industry, but by the end of the war, when almost a million women were employed in munitions, they were still paid substantially less than their male colleagues.

It is estimated that women in munitions produced 80 per cent of the shells and other weapons used by the British Army. They risked their lives every day by working with poisonous substances without adequate protective clothing or proper safety measures. The women who worked in munitions became known as 'canaries' because of the yellow tinge that skin exposed to TNT acquired. This poisonous explosive could cause a potentially fatal condition called toxic jaundice. There were also some dreadful incidents where women, as well as men, were killed in explosions in munitions factories.

In Liverpool, there were eight munitions factories: these were at Clyde Street and Brasenose Road in Bootle, the Aintree National Filling Factory, the Litherland Explosives Factory, Edge Lane and Rimrose Road, Lambeth Road Tramway Depot, where Avro Planes were also built, and the North Haymarket site, where 85 per cent of the workers were women and the factory worked around the clock. This factory was visited by King George V in 1917. In Walton, a piece of land had been bought in 1913 for £51,000 to create what became Walton Hall Park. The war delayed these plans until 1924, when the land was laid out as a park for £40,000. Meanwhile this large area was used as a munitions depot.

KIRKBY MUNITIONS
Employing about 10,000 people, of whom more than 8,000 were women, the safety record of Kirkby's munitions factory was exemplary. Even so, there were numerous injuries and some fatalities. The work involved creating volatile detonators, and women were regularly at risk of death from explosions.

CUNARD NATIONAL SHELL FACTORY, BOOTLE.
CONCERT PARTY.

Liverpool munitionettes formed the High Explosives Concert Group.

In country areas, women had always done some farm work; wives and daughters of farmers traditionally undertook dairy work and the keeping of hens, and the collection and selling of eggs. But now there was a desperate need for women to replace the number of young male farm-workers who had enlisted. In 1914, Lydiate, near Ormskirk, was a predominantly agricultural village with a population of about a thousand. There are twenty-three names on the two war memorials, of whom only a few are not listed on the 1911 census as farm labourers and these few include a coachman, a horse-man, a gardener and the son of a market gardener who worked for his father. These men, who were killed in action or died of wounds, are only a small proportion of the numbers who enlisted from this one small village, so the agricultural workforce was substantially depleted.

So there was deep concern about the nation's ability to feed itself. Many experienced agricultural workers had gone to fight and, in 1916, the wheat harvest was lower than usual. There were also problems with the potato crop in Scotland and some areas of England.

Germany was using submarine warfare to prevent British merchant ships bringing food from overseas and many ships were torpedoed. Much of the food carried never reached Britain.

The war had taken horses as well as men from the fields, thus decreasing food production. Shortages encouraged hoarding and also brought a rise in food prices; this caused hardship and, especially for poorer people, there was a real danger of malnutrition.

It became increasingly clear that some organised action should be taken. In the country areas around Liverpool, women had joined older men to work on the land since the beginning of the war, when many of the younger menfolk enlisted.

Posters told people to eat less bread in order to save the lives of British seamen, since grain for bread-making was imported. Fresh food was also in short supply, and in order to attempt to remedy this situation, many green spaces were turned into allotments that were offered to people in the local area; there were nationwide campaigns to encourage them to take up this opportunity to help feed their own families.

BRITONS! SHOULDER TO SHOULDER

Skilled Workers of Britain!

WAR MUNITION VOLUNTEERS

are wanted to stand behind our Soldiers and Sailors! If not engaged on war work already, give them your strength and your skill. *Their* duty is to fight—magnificently and heroically they do it. *Your* urgent duty is to supply them with Munitions —imperatively they are wanted.

Get into the Factory Line and help the Firing Line. Enrol to-day at the nearest Munitions Work Bureau— you will not suffer in wages, nor will your conditions of labour be prejudiced by the change.

WAR WORKERS WANTED
Skilled in the following and kindred Trades:

MILLWRIGHTS,
TOOL FITTERS,
TURNERS,
TOOL MAKERS,
FITTERS,
BOILER MAKERS,
SHIPWRIGHTS,
and other Skilled Workers in Engineering and Shipbuilding.

Apply to MUNITIONS WORK BUREAU, for full particulars. If you don't know where it is any Labour Exchange will tell you.

ENROL TO-DAY AS A WAR MUNITION VOLUNTEER

All Munitions Work Bureaux will Remain Open until Saturday, July 10th.

HOURS: 6 P.M. TO 9 P.M.   SATURDAY: 4 P.M. TO 6 P.M.

'Britons! Shoulder to Shoulder': war workers wanted.

BUY LESS MEAT.

Temporary Shortage.

In spite of the small percentage of profit added to cost, prices are unreasonably high.

Our soldiers must be well fed and the majority of available meat supplies are being diverted accordingly.

Follow our suggestion. Buy less meat. You will save money and help to bring prices down.

Coopers

CHURCH ST., LIVERPOOL.

SEND FOR COOPER'S MARKET PRICE LIST.

Telephone 4,800 Royal.

EVENING EXPRESS JUNE 5 1916 P4

Coopers of Church Street ask customers to 'Buy Less Meat'.

Some people already grew fruit and vegetables in their own garden. They were encouraged to preserve extra produce as jam, pickles or chutney so that there would be more to eat in the winter and they would reduce their demand on the food supply.

Despite these measures, it became clear that further action was needed. So, despite some reluctance, in 1918 the government introduced rationing in the hope that food would be distributed more fairly.

Sugar, meat, butter, margarine, flour and milk were all rationed so that everyone got some of what they needed. The allowance of sugar for an adult or a child was half a pound weekly; butter and margarine were 4 ounces for an adult or a child. Bread was allowed at 7 pounds per week for a man in industrial or manual

*'Strictly Legal':
a cartoon in the*
Liverpool Evening
Express, *1915.*

MAY 21 1915

6.—EVENING EXPRESS, LIVERPOOL, FRIDAY, MAY

P5

"STRICTLY LEGAL.

Hungry Boarder.—Is this a steak or a mistake?
Landlady. Government orders, sir.

[The Board of Trade to-day appeal to the public to economise on the consumption of meat.]

Land Girls kept the farms running.

work and 4 pounds for a woman in industrial work or domestic service. There was advice offered that tea should be used sparingly and that potatoes could be used freely.

The burden of managing the rationing fell on housewives, who had to register their ration cards with their shopkeepers and often still had to queue to obtain their fair share of what had arrived in the shops. Everyone had a ration card and any attempt to cheat the system could result in a fine or even imprisonment. School dinners became more widely available and were used as another way of sharing food fairly.

Those women, living in country areas or on farms, who had begun to work on the land as soon as their men left home were not enough to fill the gaps left by the men. They could not produce enough food to feed the nation. So, from 1917, the Women's Land Army (WLA) was formed to provide the extra labour to produce the food that the nation needed.

The WLA offered female labour to farmers, who were generally not very enthusiastic about employing women. The 260,000 volunteers who made up the WLA were given no real training, learning by hard-won experience and by making mistakes. They were issued with a uniform and orders to work hard. Fuel restrictions made a return to manual agricultural labour inevitable.

THE LIVERPOOL DAILY POST AND MERCURY, FRIDAY, DECEMBER 3, 1915.

WOMEN WORKERS AT LIVERPOOL POST OFFICE.

Over two hundred women are employed at the Liverpool Post Office. Our photograph shows some of them at work.

Women workers at Liverpool Post Office, December 1915.

Employing women meant that working the land was being done as cheaply as possible, and the women seem to have accepted low wages as part of their patriotic war effort.

Women had already entered the workforce in greater numbers than ever before from the beginning of the war, but many more were needed after conscription because there were even fewer workers. In 1915, the government had already asked women to register at a Labour Exchange so that they could be directed into the industrial or agricultural workforce, both of which were suffering a reduced workforce. After conscription even more women were needed and they began to do traditional men's jobs; they became firemen, coalmen and factory workers. In Liverpool, women were employed as post women. After an initial trial, over 200 women were employed by the General Post Office (GPO).

DOCKERS IN KHAKI.

Lord Derby's Novel Scheme.

BATTALION OF TRANSPORT WORKER

Increased Mobility of Labour.

Lord Derby yesterday unfolded an important scheme for relieving the congestion at the docks. He has received the permission of Lord Kitchener to raise a Dock Battalion for carrying out Government work at the port.

It is entirely his Lordship's idea, and if it is proved to be a success, it will no doubt be followed in other ports in the kingdom where similar difficulties have to be contended with.

In explaining his proposals to a number of Press representatives, Lord Derby wished it to be emphatically understood that they were in no way the outcome of the week-end strike trouble at Birkenhead, but were under his consideration long before the present state of affairs arose in Birkenhead.

All the enlisted men will be trade unionists, and they are to serve for the period of the war and for civil service only. Lord Derby is to command the battalion, and several of the union leaders are to be appointed officers.

It is not intended to use the new force as strike-breakers, but to perform necessary and urgent work. The main purpose is the provision of more mobile labour.

Dockers in khaki: mobility of labour.

Merseyside's role in shipbuilding meant that the region played a central part in the Great War. Cammell Laird in Birkenhead was playing its part in production. The Royal Navy cruisers *Birkenhead*, *Chester*, *Caroline*, *Castor*, *Caledon*, *Cairo*, *Constance* and *Capetown* were all built there and launched on the mighty Mersey.

The import and export of goods was also crucial, but about 800 Liverpool dockers had enlisted and therefore the shipping lines were obliged to look for substitute labour. One of the first to try introducing female porters and warehouse workers was the Harrison line. But most dock workers refused to work with women and the attempt at introducing women workers in the docks failed. However, dock work was particularly heavy and dangerous, so it seems likely that few women would have been physically strong enough to undertake it, especially at that time.

THE HARRISON LINE

The origins of the Harrison line lay with two brothers, Thomas and James, who began their employment at Samuel Brown, which was a company of Liverpool shipbrokers. In 1839 Thomas became a partner in the firm, and in 1849 James joined him. The firm was mainly concerned at this stage with importing brandy and wine from the Charente Valley and the town of Cognac in France.

In 1853, the Harrison brothers took over the company following the death of George Brown. They began their early shipping empire exclusively in sail, with a fleet size of approximately thirty to forty ships. Their first screw-propelled steamers were added to the fleet in 1860 and the steamer side of the business then began to expand very quickly, although they did continue to acquire sailing ships until 1874. Thomas Harrison moved from the centre of Liverpool to the substantial Moss Side House in Park Lane, Maghull.

The Harrisons entered the Great War with fifty-five ships. During the war they lost twenty-seven vessels, but because they continued to build new ships, the fleet remained at forty vessels by the end of 1917. The Harrisons' line received about £3 million in compensation for the lost vessels. It cost them about £4,800,000 to replace their losses between 1918 and 1920. The Moss Side Hospital, originally intended as a hospital to treat epilepsy, became a centre that pioneered treatment for shell shock. The site incorporated two farms and Moss Side House, the mansion built in the 1830s for Thomas Harrison. So this military hospital, which had originally been the home of the Liverpool merchant, became indirectly another contribution of the Harrison line to the war effort.

One of the visible signs of changing times must have been the appearance of women police officers during the Great War, although they were called Women's Patrols. Their main duty was to control and supervise women's behaviour near factories or hostels. There was still a Victorian attitude that suggested certain classes or ages of women were too silly to behave sensibly without supervision. Evidence of this attitude is the fact that one of the duties of these patrols was to search women to ensure that they did not take anything into the factories that was likely to cause an explosion. Women's Patrols were also seen in parks and railway stations and near public houses.

New opportunities for women became available in public transport. Women began working as bus conductresses, sometimes known as conductorettes. This aspect of women's war service was seen in the long-running television programme *Upstairs, Downstairs*, when Rose, a house parlourmaid, became a conductorette, in addition to her role in service. Although fictional, the degree of freedom that she enjoyed in her work in public transport, in contrast with her former restricted lifestyle, was apparent. Women also became porters, ticket collectors, omnibus, tram and railway carriage cleaners, and even bus drivers. During the Great War, the number of women working on the railways rose to 50,000 from under 10,000.

Flowers of France

Gathered for you

Embroidered postcards sent to mothers, wives and sweethearts.

The Separation Allowance, an allocation of money to the wife of a man serving his country, was very low and there was considerable discussion in the newspapers as to whether the money was misspent, particularly on drink. The Women's Patrols near public houses were alerted to this perceived problem. However, there must have been many respectable women of whom the courts and the press never heard who were finding it difficult to manage when their menfolk enlisted or were conscripted.

Women with children who needed to become employed outside the home must have found that the care of their young children could be a problem. Even in times when young children were left routinely in the charge of sisters not much older than themselves, and when tight-knit communities existed where neighbours and other family members would care for children who were left alone, there were some infants who needed a more formal arrangement. The government wanted women to work in munitions, so it was obliged to provide some funds towards the cost of day nurseries for munitions workers. By 1917, there were over a hundred day nurseries across the country. However, there was still no provision for women working in any other form of employment and they still had to rely on friends and family to help care for their children while they were at work.

Some women were keen to assist the war effort and become more involved in the war; there was pressure for their own uniformed service, which began in August 1914. The War Office investigated and realised that many jobs being done by soldiers in France could instead be done by women, thus releasing the men for front-line duties. In December 1916, the Women's Army Auxiliary Corps (WAAC) was established. It was later renamed Queen Mary's Army Auxiliary Corps. The Women's Royal Naval Service was formed in November 1917 and the Women's Royal Air Force was set up on 1 April 1918. In total, over 100,000 women joined Britain's armed forces during the war.

Women replaced male soldiers in offices, canteens, transport roles, stores and army bases. WAAC volunteers wore a green or 'khaki' uniform like male soldiers. It included a small cap, khaki jacket and skirt. The skirt had to be no more than 12in from the ground. Women in the WAAC exercised every day, taking part in Morris dancing and hockey to keep fit.

By 1916, some women had been working with mechanics and gained sufficient skill to be able to undertake the task of repairing motor vehicles that had broken down. Women repaired trucks and also built new ones in factories. This was one of the areas of work for women that would never have been imagined before the war.

There were some traditional women's tasks that now found a new application in a war situation. One of the most important jobs women did was to cook for men in camps and hospitals. Women looked after soldiers by cooking wholesome food such as stew, fish cakes and liver and onions. They also made beef tea, mutton broth, brawn, potato pie and stodgy, filling puddings. The food was intended to bulk up the calories that the men consumed. Men at war consumed an estimated 4,600 calories a day, compared with a working man's 3,400 a day at home. Feeding the troops was intended to go some way to remedying the situation that had been discovered when they enlisted – that many were ill-nourished or under-nourished.

Much of the food that was offered to the troops was better quality than the food they had eaten back home. It was also likely to be in greater amounts than they had been used to. The canteen cooks had instructions to make the food feed as many men as possible, so they used various methods to make the supplies go further. They might dip rashers of bacon into oatmeal to make them more filling. Oatmeal could also be used to make stews and pie fillings more substantial. Stale bread could be soaked in water and baked again in the oven to make it more palatable and to save waste.

One form of work that was seen as more acceptable for women was office work – particularly for young ladies who might not have worked outside the home before the war, but who now wanted to contribute to the war effort. Lord Derby's call to arms had specifically targeted young male office workers, so in the Liverpool area there were many clerical and administrative vacancies for women. Typically, women received 24s per week for unskilled work, but higher rates were paid for positions that called for skills like shorthand or typing that had required training.

Nursing was already an area of service that seemed appropriate for women, but now it attracted all social classes, including young women who would previously have been seen as unlikely to cope with its less pleasant aspects. There were a number of military hospitals in the Liverpool area. Some were purpose built; many were wings of existing hospitals or newly adapted buildings.

In 1914, the War Office accepted an offer from Lord Derby of Knowsley Hall as a 120-bed base hospital. There was also the Lord Derby War Hospital, which was situated north of Warrington, Lancashire. It had been built in 1896, but was now used as a military hospital with about 3,000 beds. Between 1915 and 1920 over 56,000 wounded soldiers were treated there. From 1916, there was treatment of mental patients, and although this was the hospital's original purpose, many of those classified in this way were former soldiers with head injuries or shell shock. The hospital returned completely to its origins as an asylum in 1921.

All of Lord Derby's family were involved in the war effort; the *Liverpool Daily Post* made an announcement on 27 July 1917 that the Countess of Derby had given a fully furnished wing of Knowsley Hall to provide a convalescent hospital for female munitions workers from the Liverpool area. Nurses from the Voluntary Aid Detachment (VAD) were to staff the wing and a fund of private subscriptions had been set up to enable local women to benefit from the care and recuperation available at the hall. In early August, the wing was opened with a dozen patients. An application in writing had to be made by the women, their families or their employers for admission. There was a charge of 10s per week. The surroundings must have been as unfamiliar to most of these young women as the stately homes in which wounded working-class soldiers were finding themselves.

> **ONE OF MANY LIVERPOOL NURSES**
> The *Liverpool Echo*, 24 February 1917, reported that Sister Beatrice Stanhope Tinkler, daughter of Mr and Mrs George Tinkler of 72, Devonshire Road, Liverpool had been awarded Royal Red Cross Class 2 for her nursing service in base hospitals, stationary hospitals, casualty clearing stations and ambulance trains. 'Many have been grateful for her kindly care and skill throughout the war.'

'We Mean to Fight It Through': sheet music was very popular.

Other prominent citizens also offered their houses, including the offer by the trustees of the late Sir Alfred Jones to use his house Oaklands in the Aigburth-Garston area as a military hospital. This building stood in a large estate with substantial gardens. Again, the contrast for wounded soldiers, not only with the horrors of the battlefields, but also with their own homes, must have been remarkable.

Hospital for wounded soldiers, Woolton Road.

There were numerous other military hospitals on Merseyside. These included Toxteth Park Military Hospital; a General Hospital in Fazakerley; and the Alder Hey Orthopaedic Hospital, which was a military unit treating cases that had not been not sent to the Royal National Orthopaedic Hospital in London. At Alder Hey, there was also a special unit for limbless men from Cheshire and Lancashire.

The huge involvement of Lord Derby, his family and his estates meant that Knowsley Hall knew many guises during the war. It was a military hospital and a convalescent home for women munitions workers, and it was also a training camp for the Liverpool Pals. In the Deer Park, covering almost 600 acres, a military camp was situated and an area of parkland in Eccleston was also given over for the same purpose.

As well as a number of other battalions from other local regiments stationed at Knowsley Park, including the East Lancashire Regiment and the

SIR ALFRED JONES
Sir Alfred, owner of a Liverpool shipping line, had been instrumental in founding the Liverpool School of Tropical Medicine. Chairman of the Bank of British West Africa, president of the British Cotton Growing Association and president of the Liverpool Chamber of Commerce, Sir Alfred died in 1909, leaving large charitable bequests.

Liverpool Pals, 1914.

Cheshire Regiment, there were the Pals battalions, the 17th, 18th, 19th and 20th battalions of the King's Liverpool Regiment, known as the 1st, 2nd, 3rd and 4th Liverpool Pals. Most of them came from Liverpool and the surrounding area. They had been given the silver cap badge featuring the crest of the Stanley family, the Eagle and Child, bearing the motto, 'Sans Changer', meaning 'Without Change'.

There were wooden huts, which were preferable to tents, where the men slept; there were adequate washing and laundry facilities, and entertainment was provided on the site, including a theatre. Some of the men were probably more comfortable than they had been at home. The Young Men's Christian Association (YMCA) was also involved in providing entertainment and nourishing meals. There were regular appeals from soldiers in the local press for items for use in the camps, such as gramophone records and sports equipment.

Training for warfare was not always what some men might have expected. For instance, Lord Derby's brother, Brigadier Stanley, in charge of the Pals battalions, thought the men who had not previously had jobs requiring manual labour needed practice in digging trenches, so Lord Derby gave permission for this activity to take place on his land. Some of the men felt that they were merely clearing land for the benefit of the estate. But the benefit was shared because the grounds of Knowsley Hall were used to cultivate crops which helped the local community with the serious food shortages later in the war.

However, on 29 April 1915, the Pals left Knowsley Park to go to Grantham for military training. From early morning, crowds were gathering at Prescot station to give the troops a rousing send-off. Eight trains departed every hour from early morning from the station. Later, the brigade moved to Salisbury Plain, before embarkation in October to France. Lady Derby immediately formed a fundraising committee to provide comforts to the Pals. There is no doubt that Lady Derby supplemented her husband's efforts in many ways for the welfare of the people.

Before the departure, a Grand Military Gymkhana was held at Knowsley Park, when the public were invited to spend a day with the Pals. There were various attractions, including a display

The Kaiser Wants You to Stay at Home'.

with over a thousand men from the cavalry and artillery taking part. There was a military band and a torchlight tattoo. It was an impressive and inspiring sight, obviously intended to boost recruitment as well as morale; men were strongly persuaded to enlist on the day and be fully equipped to take part in the March Past Parade, taken by Lord Derby.

Nevertheless, by spring 1915 the flow of volunteer recruits had greatly reduced and it became clear that the number of men who would be needed for the war could not be supplied by voluntary recruitment. The upper age limit for recruitment was raised to 40 in May 1915.

On 15 July 1915, the government passed the National Registration Act. It was intended to ascertain how many men between the ages of 15 and 65 were engaged in various trades. All those in this age range who had not already enlisted were obliged to register, giving their employment details. The results of this census became available by mid-September 1915: it showed there were almost 5 million males of military age who were not in the forces, of which about 1.5 million men were in scarce or skilled occupations.

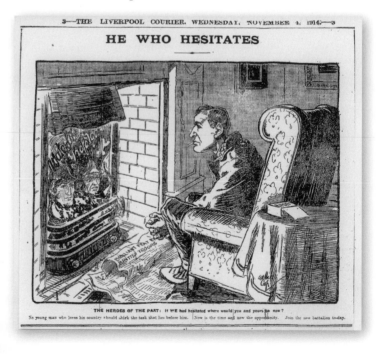

*'He Who Hesitates'
reminds men of past
British victories.*

LIVERPOOL, TUESDAY, FEBRUARY 2, 1915.—5

SIX SONS IN THE NAVY.

Mrs. Ellen Nicol, of 15, Morley-street, Kirkdale, had the proud distinction of having six sons serving in the Navy at the outbreak of war, but one, Walter, the youngest, was lost in the sinking of H.M.S. Aboukir. The five others are on board different ships, as indicated (left to right):— William (H.M.S. Powerful), Edward (H.M.S. Essex), Richard (H.M.S. Indefatigable), John (H.M.S. Torpay), James (H.M.S. Brilliant), Walter (H.M.S. Aboukir). Mrs. Ellen Nicol (who is seen in the centre of the group) has received the following letter, together with a silver memento:—"The keeper of the Privy Purse presents his compliments to Mrs. Nicol, and is commanded by the King to say that his Majesty has heard with the deepest gratification that she has had six sons serving in the Navy. The King sends Mrs. Nicol his congratulations, and desires that she will convey the same to her sons, together with his Majesty's best wishes for their success, health, and happiness in the noble career they have chosen."

'Six Sons in the Navy' sets a patriotic example.

2.—EXPRESS, LIVERPOOL, SATURDAY, FEBRUARY

EXAMPLE OF ELEVEN OF 'EM!

'Eleven of 'Em', Liverpool Express, 1916.

Great Patriotic Labour Demonstration.

A Great Demonstration will be held in

SHEIL PARK,

On SUNDAY, JULY 29th, 1917,

(Under the auspices of the Liverpool Branch of The British Workers' League)

"To repudiate the resolutions passed in the name of Labour by the Bogus Pacifists' Conference at Leeds, and to declare the unalterable adhesion of the workers of Liverpool to the Allied cause and the principle of an Allied Victory."

Meeting will commence at 3 p.m. prompt.

Speakers—

(1) **David Gilmour,** Scottish Miners' Federation.
A. McLeod, N. U. D. L. and R. W.
A. T. Abrahamson, N.U. Ship Stewards, Cooks and Bakers.
Chairman—J. SEXTON, J.P., C.C., Vice-President Nat. Transport Workers' Fed.

Speakers—

(2) **J. J. Terrett,** N.U. General Workers, London.
A. Short, Seamen's Insurance, Liverpool.
E. Tomkinson, Mr. Hughes, Discharged Soldiers' and
Sailors' Federation.
F. Hodson, N. U. D. L. & R. W.
Chairman—J. WOOD, N. U. D. L. and R. W.

Speakers—

(3) **G. Milligan,** N. U. D. L. and R. W.
J. Riley, Liverpool. **T. Williamson,** N. A. U. Labour.
F. A. Baker (Wire Drawers), Warrington.
Chairman—T. DUNFORD, N. U. D. L. and R. W.

Speakers—

(4) **J. A. Seddon,** Chairman General Council B. W. L.
G. Wood, President Mersey Quay and Railway Carters' Union.
H. H. Duke, India Rubber Workers and Asbestos Workers,
Manchester.
D. O'Hare, N. U. D. L. and R. W.
Chairman—T. DONNELLY, N. U. Ship Stewards, Cooks and Bakers.

Also J. McNamara, N. U. D. L. and R. W.; E. Wright, Warrington; J. Eaton, India Rubber Workers, Warrington; Alfred Devalve, N. U. D. L. and R. W.; Major Thompson, Birkenhead; T. Crawford, Wigan.

WORKERS OF LIVERPOOL! Roll up in your thousands, irrespective of Party or Creed, and by your presence show your unabated confidence in the great cause of the Allied Nations!

Join the British Workers' League, 1s. per year.
Buy the "British Citizen," 1d. per week.

The Labour movement asserts its loyalty.

The government was still unwilling to move directly to compulsory military service, so it was decided to try another method of enlistment.

This was officially called the Group Scheme but it rapidly became known as the Derby Scheme, because on 11 October 1915 Lord Derby was appointed Director-General of Recruiting. He had played a major and highly successful role in raising volunteers, especially for the King's (Liverpool) Regiment; now he was to lead a national effort to raise recruitment numbers.

The new programme was introduced by Lord Derby five days after his appointment. Men aged 18 to 40 were informed that under the scheme they could continue to enlist voluntarily or attest with an obligation to come if called up later on. The War Office notified the public that voluntary enlistment would soon cease and that the last day of registration would be 15 December 1915.

Men who attested under the Derby Scheme could be accepted for service, but could choose to defer it. They were listed as Class A, whereas those who agreed to immediate service were Class B. The Class A men were paid a day's army pay for the day on which they attested. They were given a grey armband with a red crown as a sign that they had volunteered and were officially transferred into Section B Army Reserve. Then they were able to return to their usual employment until they were called up.

4

NEWS FROM THE FRONT LINE

There were men from Liverpool engaged in all aspects of the front line, and women, too, not so far behind the lines. There were thousands of men at the front; there were men in the Royal Navy and men in the Mercantile Marine; there were even men in the Royal Flying Corps – some of them were very young men, like Ewan Blackledge.

Ewan lived at Rose Hill, Pygons Hill Lane, Lydiate, a substantial house on the outskirts of a rural village. He was the son of James and Lucy Elizabeth Mary Blackledge and had two brothers and three sisters. The Blackledge family were well-known

Rose Hill, Pygons Hill Lane, Lydiate: home of the Blackledge family.

Liverpool bakers with a factory and a number of shops and Ewan had enjoyed a privileged education at Ampleforth, where he was a member of the Officer Training Corps.

Ewan was only 15 in 1914, but he went to Sandhurst as soon as he could do so and was in the King's (Liverpool) Regiment. He transferred to the Royal Flying Corps and was shot down on a reconnaissance flight on 27 November 1917 by Lothar, a younger brother of the Red Baron, Manfred von Richthofen.

Ewan Blackledge at Ampleforth.

Ewan Blackledge

Age: 20. Died: 27th November 1917.
Lieutenant Ewan Blackledge is perhaps the best known of those men from Lydiate who were killed in the Great War.

The Blackledge family were well-known Liverpool bakers with a factory and dozens of shops. The family business was founded by Ewan's father James Blackledge in the 1840s.

Ewan lived at Rose Hill, Pygons Hill Lane with James and Lucy Blackledge and their two other sons and three daughters.

He was educated at Ampleforth boarding school in North Yorkshire, where he was a member of the Officer Training Corps.

He went to the Royal Military Academy Sandhurst in Berkshire before joining The King's (Liverpool) Regiment, later being transferred to the Royal Flying Corps. He was shot down on a reconnaissance flight on 27th November 1917.

Lieutenant Ewan Blackledge.

LOTHAR VON RICHTHOFEN

Lothar-Siegfried von Richthofen was a German fighter ace, who was credited with forty victories, although some of these are dubious. Lothar was a younger brother of Manfred von Richthofen, known as the Red Baron. He was also a cousin of Luftwaffe Field Marshal Wolfram von Richthofen.

Lothar was born in1894. Like his brother Manfred, Lothar began the war as a cavalry officer with the 4th Dragoon Regiment. In October 1914, while stationed at Attigny, he was awarded the Iron Cross 2nd Class for valour. He joined the *Luftstreitkräfte* – the German Army Air Service – in 1915.

He won the Iron Cross 1st Class in December 1916, and then began training as a pilot.

He was credited with shooting down the British air ace, Captain Albert Ball, but the evidence suggests that, in fact, Ball crashed and the claim that he had been shot down was propaganda. Richthofen had claimed that he had brought down a Sopwith Triplane, which was not Ball's plane. There was no battle damage to Ball's plane and the doctor who examined Ball reported massive injuries from the crash, but no bullet wounds. However, the propaganda value of Ball's death under the guns of a German pilot was obvious, and the Germans awarded Lothar a victory over Ball.

Lothar was wounded in the hip by anti-aircraft fire and crash-landed on 13 May 1917. On 14 May he was awarded the Pour le Mérite; his injuries kept him out of combat for five months and he returned to active service in September.

He is believed to have shot down Ewan Blackledge, of Lydiate, who was on a reconnaissance flight, on 27 November 1917.

Signallers, King's (Liverpool) Regiment, 1916.

The Liverpool Pals battalions were involved in most of the major actions of the war, but there were Liverpool men in several other regiments of the King's (Liverpool) and other regiments too.

The Liverpool Scottish is a unit of the British Army, part of the Army Reserve, which had been the Territorial Army. The Liverpool Scottish came into being in 1900, when it was an infantry battalion of the King's (Liverpool) Regiment. When war was declared in August 1914, the Liverpool Scottish mobilised and moved to Scotland under the command of Lieutenant-Colonel William Nicholl. The first battalion was well trained compared with most other territorial units and volunteered for overseas service. It became the seventh territorial battalion to be dispatched to the Western Front.

More than 10,000 men served with the Scottish and about 1,000, a tenth of those who served, died during the war. Their first major battle was on 16 June 1915 at Bellewaarde, known

...TISER, THURSDAY AFTERNOON, MAY 13, 1915.

G. R.

To the MEN of Lancashire.

LIVERPOOL SCOTTISH.

YOU are wanted at once for FOREIGN SERVICE in the 10th (Scottish) Battalion " The King's " Liverpool Regiment.

Certainty of seeing ACTIVE SERVICE.

JOIN NOW. Do you fully realise that we British to-day are fighting for our very lives; and that a failure in this conflict with Germany will mean, not merely decrease of wages and curtailment of freedom, but bitter ruin, shame, outrage, and desolation to every single home and farmstead ?

Remember Belgium's horrible fate, and the British womenfolk and babies foully murdered on the Lusitania and elsewhere. See to it now that your own mothers, sisters, wives and children shall not meet with a like fate.

Apply at Depot, **LIVERPOOL SCOTTISH,**
7, FRASER STREET, LIVERPOOL.

Qualifications—

Age 19 to 38. Minimum height 5 ft. 4 ins. Minimum chest (expanded) 34 ins.
Subscription suspended during the War.

my20

The Liverpool Scottish Battalion recruitment appeal.

LIVERPOOL'S SCROLL OF FAME.

Captain NOEL GODFREY CHAVASSE, V.C. and Bar,

10th (Scottish) Battalion,

THE KING'S (LIVERPOOL REGIMENT).

THE brief but very impressive life and death story of Captain Noel Godfrey Chavasse, V.C., of the R.A.M.C., will ever stand in the forefront of the war annals of Liverpool, and deserves to be written in letters of gold on imperishable marble as an everlasting example to successive generations of Britain's youth of highmindedness, conscientious devotion to duty, superb personal bravery, and a ready and constant self-sacrifice even unto death. He was of the highest type of England's young manhood—a brilliant scholar and a fine athlete, clean in mind and body, a Christian gentleman well equipped for life's battle, possessing a rare sense of the brotherhood of the human race, and standing at the threshold of what, without doubt, would have been a great career as a healer of men's bodies and builder-up of men's souls and characters.

Such a man was he when the bugle of war sounded, and then in the fiery furnace of conflict his personality proved itself as finest steel, casting lustre on his race, his ancestry, his education and his environment. He did a man's part in the trenches and in No Man's Land; he ministered tirelessly and with absolute self-forgetfulness to the wounded; and in the end gave his life for his comrades.

Captain Chavasse was a son of Oxford by birth and educational training, but Liverpool, too, had a considerable part in the moulding of his character, for he came here as a boy when his father became the Bishop of Liverpool, studied for a time at Liverpool College, and began the practice of his profession first as house physician and afterwards as house surgeon at the Royal Southern Hospital. While at Trinity College, Oxford, he had a notable career, and having graduated with class honours took his medical degrees at Oxford and London. He was an accomplished athlete, and won his Oxford "blue" at the same time as his twin brother. He and his brother were keen competitors in the 100 yards and the quarter mile, while both represented Oxford successfully against the sprinters of Cambridge. He excelled also in Rugby Football and Lacrosse, and played both games for his University.

Although Captain Chavasse was a student of Oxford, and took the degree of that University, a considerable part of his studies was carried out at the University of Liverpool. It is a testimony to his keenness that he took vacation courses during the years 1905—1909, and thereafter until 1912 was a regular student. He held the Derby Exhibition, which is awarded for clinical work, and after qualifying he became one of the resident medical officers at the Royal Southern Hospital, where a brass tablet to his memory has been placed in the main corridor.

Liverpool generally knew next to nothing of this splendid young fellow until his name began to appear in the dispatches and honours list. He had already begun to take life and citizenship seriously, and was making good use of his leisure time. From boyhood he had dreamed of becoming a medical missionary, and such a bent found a natural outlet in work for the moral betterment of the boys of Grafton Street Industrial Schools, among whom he worked for some time modestly

and successfully. Of this phase of his life we are given a vivid glimpse in a letter he wrote to a regimental comrade on November 2nd, 1916, just after the award to him of the V.C. "I look back," he wrote, "on the work in the Industrial School as a great turning point in my life. It made me realise how well off I was and what others suffered cheerfully." The work developed his communal conscience, but did not destroy his native modesty. And so it was all through. It was of others and the good they did him that he spoke, never realizing, as the friend referred to has put on record, that it was his own character and example and the charm of his personality that constituted the magnetism that bound him so closely to those among whom he moved and worked.

"His relationship to the Industrial School boys," we read, "was precisely similar to that which endeared him to his regiment. He became one of them; he lived among them during their annual camp at Hightown. He taught them the principles of sport, impressing on them how to comport themselves in a gentlemanly way towards their rivals. He founded a society among the boys which largely helped to increase the existing tone in the school, with its results of high ideals of purity, truth, integrity, and morality, which have led those who have left school to take honourable places in the industrial world, and this school can always be trusted to turn out reliable boys."

It was work like this—as well as his hospital duties—that young Dr. Chavasse left behind him at the call of King and Country in the autumn of 1914.

Noel Chavasse, Double VC.

as the Battle of Hooge. This action was intended to pin down German reserves while other Allied forces were engaged elsewhere. Hooge is a village near the much better known Ypres, in Belgium.

The best-known soldier of the Liverpool Scottish during the war was Captain Noel Godfrey Chavasse, who was awarded two Victoria Crosses while attached from the Royal Army Medical Corps. Chavasse remains one of only three people to have been awarded the VC twice, and the only recipient from the Liverpool Scottish.

Noel Chavasse was the son of the Bishop of Liverpool, Francis Chavasse. The family lived in Abercromby Square, where there is now a memorial statue to Noel. A soldier from Liverpool, who witnessed him in action, said of Noel that the VC 'was too small a reward for such a man'. He won the Military Cross in 1915 near Ypres and his first VC at the Battle of the Somme in 1916. His second VC, awarded posthumously, was won at Passchendaele, the Third Battle of Ypres.

Noel was an award-winning academic, and had qualified as a doctor. Alongside his twin brother, Christopher, he had represented Great Britain when they ran together at the 1908 Olympics. Like many young men, he had joined the fighting eagerly, writing: 'I envy Chris going off so soon.' But later, like others, he changed his view, having seen so much bitter fighting and suffering. In 1916, he wrote, 'It is only the faces of the men that keep me anxious to help them at all times.'

His brother, Christopher Chavasse, won the Military Cross and was later awarded the OBE. He became Bishop of Rochester and lived to 1962.

Sergeant Albert Baybut, Chavasse's medical orderly, is, strictly, the most highly decorated soldier in the history of Liverpool Scottish because Chavasse's unit was actually the Royal Army Medical Corps (RAMC). Baybut received a Distinguished Conduct Medal, and Bar, together with the Military Medal for his actions alongside Chavasse during the First World War.

The second-line battalion became responsible for the training of recruits and provision of drafts for overseas service.

The Liverpool Irish enter Lille, 18 October 1918.

It was committed to the Western Front in 1917. The third-line remained in Britain for the duration of the war.

The battalion's original strength – those who qualified for the 1914 Star – became known as the Maidaners, a reference to SS *Maidan*, the vessel on which they sailed to war. The 1914 Star, sometimes called the Mons Star, was a campaign medal awarded to those who served in Belgium or France between 5 August and 22 November 1914.

Trench warfare in a severe winter soon depleted the strength of the Liverpool Scottish. The battalion had reduced in numbers from 26 officers and 829 men recorded in November to only 370 able-bodied men by January 1915. Within weeks of the battalion's arrival, Major Blair, Lieutenant-Colonel Nicholl's successor, was replaced by J.R. Davidson due to ill-health. Davidson commanded the battalion, despite being wounded during the Somme offensive, until 1917, when he returned to Liverpool to become the city's chief engineer.

In the final months of the war leading up to the armistice of 11 November 1918, the Liverpool Scottish helped to secure numerous villages without opposition and crossed the River Scheldt on 9 November. On the day of the armistice, the Liverpool Scottish was situated at Villers-Notre-Dame.

The Liverpool Irish is one of the units of the British Army's Territorial Army; it was raised in 1860 as a volunteer corps of infantry and became a battalion of the King's (Liverpool) Regiment in July 1881. During the Great War, it suffered thousands of casualties in numerous battles including Givenchy, Guillemont, the Third Battle of Ypres, and the Hundred Days Offensive. The Liverpool Irish were disbanded after the Great War in 1922, but reformed in 1939.

The regiment asserted their Irish heritage in their traditions and uniform. They originally adopted a uniform which was similar in appearance to the Royal Irish Rifles, but later they wore the caubeen headdress with red and blue hackle, while the attire of the battalion pipers included the saffron kilt and shawl. While the battalion derived pride from its Irish identity, some people, including the Earl of Derby, associated Irish identity with a lack of discipline and insubordination, for which the Liverpool Irish gained a reputation. Notwithstanding, the Liverpool Irish made a gallant and valuable contribution to the war effort.

In August 1914, at the outbreak of the Great War, the Liverpool Irish mobilised and moved to Canterbury, in Kent. Two further battalions of the regiment were raised in October 1914 and May 1915. It was during an action in 1916 that the raid's only fatality, Edward Felix Baxter, displayed such courage that he was awarded the Victoria Cross.

Edward Felix Baxter, VC

(18 September 1885–18 April 1916)

Second Lieutenant E.F. Baxter, VC, 1/8th (Irish) Battalion, The King's (Liverpool) Regiment, was the son of Charles and Beatrice Baxter. He was not from Liverpool, being born in Worcestershire and educated at Hartlebury Grammar School and Christ's Hospital. He joined the Liverpool Irish because he was teaching at Skerry's College in Liverpool when the Great War began.

He was a keen sportsman, a member of the Liverpool Motor Club and also the Westmorland and Coventry & Warwickshire clubs. He had taken part at Brooklands in the Tourist Trophy Race and had won several cups and medals in other events. In 1913, he won the Liverpool Auto Cycle Club's Reliability Trials. Because he was a skilful sporting motorcyclist, he originally enlisted as a despatch rider. He was commissioned in September 1915. During a trench raid near Blairville on the night of 17–18 April 1916, Baxter led the storming party, which was known as the 'Forty Thieves', with great courage. He led the attack into the German trench, where he shot a sentry and then helped to bomb German dugouts. He was last seen alive assisting the last of his men back over the parapet. He was posthumously awarded the Victoria Cross. King George V presented Baxter's widow with his VC at an investiture held at Buckingham Palace on 29 November 1916. He had a young daughter called Leonora.

The following is an extract from a contemporary press report, headed 'Loss to motoring':

Lieutenant Felix Edward, who has been reported missing after an attack on the German trenches, was probably the best known competition rider in or round Liverpool, and with his wife was to be found at every motor-cyclists function. He was specially trained as a bombing officer, which would no doubt appeal to his sporting instincts, and after a trench attack he did not return with his men. He figured in many races at New Brighton.

The King's (Liverpool) Regiment totalled forty-nine battalions. Twenty-six battalions served abroad and were awarded fifty-eight Battle Honours and six Victoria Crosses for service on the Western Front, in the Balkans, India, and Russia, but the regiment lost many men during the course of the war.

About 14,000 Kingsmen died during the Great War, with many thousands more injured, diseased or taken prisoner. Those who were wounded were often disabled for life with loss of limb or loss of sight.

The 1st King's was involved in the action at Mons, and at Ypres during the Race to the Sea. In the defence of Polygon Wood, the 1st King's played a vital role, decimating the 3rd Prussian Foot Guards with concentrated rapid-fire and artillery support. But there was a great cost; by the battle's end, the 1st King's casualties were enormous with more than 800 dead, both officers and men. There were numerous other engagements with the enemy and on 24 October 1914 Lieutenant-Colonel Bannatyne was killed by a sniper.

By the end of March 1915, the King's had eight battalions on the Western Front. On 24 April, the Second Ypres began. After the regiment's involvement there ended, four battalions of the King's fought at Festubert. They suffered more than 1,200 casualties. Lance Corporal Tombs became the regiment's first Victoria Cross recipient of the war for assisting wounded soldiers during the battle.

Lance Corporal Joseph Harcourt Tombs was in the 1st Battalion, King's (Liverpool) Regiment, when, the citation for his VC reads, on 16 May 1915, near Rue du Bois:

> on his own initiative he crawled out repeatedly under a very heavy shell and machine-gun fire, to bring in wounded men, who were lying about 100 yards in front of our trenches. He rescued four men, one of whom he dragged back by means of a rifle sling placed round his own neck and the man's body. This man was so severely wounded that unless he had been immediately attended to he must have died.

Joseph Tombs was invested with his Victoria Cross by King George V at Buckingham Palace on 12 August 1915. Following this action, the battalion had 400 men killed, wounded and missing, with only two of twenty-four officers present surviving and unscathed.

When the British instigated a new offensive on 25 September, at Loos, the King's were represented in the offensive by eight battalions, from standard infantry to pioneers. Chlorine gas was used on the first day of the battle, when strong winds blew the gas backwards, hindering the advance of the 1st King's. They also had to cope with the hazard of uncut barbed wire. The advance of the 9th King's also came to a halt, although they were able to capture about 300 German prisoners. More battalions were deployed before the end of the year; these included the 17th, 18th, 19th and 20th Liverpool Pals.

West Lancashire Territorials recruit for the King's (Liverpool) Regiment.

The name of (Benjamin) Arthur Jackson is recorded on the Boundary Street East Primitive Methodist Memorial and also on the Thiepval Memorial. He was killed on 1 July 1916 at the Battle of Albert, the opening battle of a series that was to become known as the Battle of the Somme. Arthur was a private in the King's (Liverpool) Regiment.

The Somme was the first mass offensive mounted by the British Expeditionary Force (BEF); it was also the first battle to involve a large number of New Army (wartime) divisions, including many Pals battalions. The Liverpool Pals' first battle came during the Big Push on 1 July 1916, the first day of the Battle of the Somme; it was the worst single day for casualties in British military history and Arthur Jackson was just one of their number. Arthur was single, an assistant in an engineer's shop, who lived in Harebell Street with his father and mother, Joseph and Sarah, and his two sisters, Annie and Nellie.

WEST LANCASHIRE TERRITORIALS

Out of 12 Battalions of this Division 9 are already at the Front, and the remaining 3 are under orders to proceed there immediately.

It is essential that the Reserve Battalions shall be kept up to full strength, and

RECRUITS ARE URGENTLY REQUIRED

DO NOT LET YOUR COMRADES AT THE FRONT REPROACH YOU FOR WANT OF SUPPORT.

Recruits for the 5th, 6th, 7th, and 9th Battalion The King's (Liverpool Regiment) will be taken either at the Recruiting Depot, Cooper's Buildings, Church-street, Liverpool, from 9 o'clock onwards each day, or at the Headquarters of these Battalions:—

5th Battalion—St. Anne-st., Liverpool.
6th Battalion—Upper Warwick-street, Liverpool.
7th Battalion—Park-street, Bootle.
9th Battalion—Everton-road, Liverpool.

Recruits for the 8th Battalion and 10th Battalion will be taken at the Headquarters of these units:—

8th Battalion—Shaw-street, Liverpool.
10th Battalion—Fraser-st., Liverpool.

DERBY

CHAIRMAN,
WEST LANCASHIRE ASSOCIATION.

BOOTLE SWIMMING CLUB.

A SCORE OF MEMBERS WITH THE COLOURS.

The annual general meeting of the club was held at the Baths on Friday, Major W. Taylor presiding.

The report of the hon. secretary (Mr. T. W. Jones) was as follows :—The season 1914, which gave promise of satisfactory results, was interrupted by the war, and consequently all events scheduled to take place after July had to be cancelled. Many members of the club had responded to the country's call, several of whom have already seen active service. The following is a list of those members who have enlisted, together with their rank, so far as is known :—

Private J. M. Kay (Liverpool Scottish).
Rifleman T. McLean (Liverpool 6th Rifles).
Rifleman H. Y. Johnson (Liverpool 6th Rifles).
Corporal E. V. Edwards (2nd Liverpool City).
Private J. Charters (Liverpool Scottish).
Sergeant A. T. Finnie (Liverpool Scottish).
Sergeant J. Irving (Liverpool Scottish).
Private T. Livesley (Liverpool Scottish).
Private R. Dowling (Gordon Highlanders).
Private E. Mason (Irish Dragoon Guards).
Private A. Robinson (2nd Liverpool City).
Private F. Mall (3rd Liverpool City).
Gunner J. D. Sutton (West Lancashire Artillery).
Gunner T. Evans (Lancashire Field Artillery).
Private T. Williamson (R.A.M.C., T.F.).
Private H. Williams (R.A.M.C., T.F.).
Sergeant S. Donaldson (R.A.M.C.).
Private Geo. Singleton (Lancashire Hussars).
Private F. Toolan (Liverpool City).
Private R. D. Milles (Liverpool Scottish).
Rifleman J. C. Potter (Liverpool 6th Rifles).

Bottle Swimming Club depleted by enlistment.

Four battalions, including three from the Liverpool Pals, attacked Guillemont on 30 July 1916. It was a dreadful event as, hampered by the fog, the British advanced toward the enemy, who, knowing where they were, could fire randomly into the advancing soldiers.

One of the Liverpool Pals killed was Lance Corporal Stephen Atherton, formerly a player, but later the groundsman for Oxton Cricket Club in Birkenhead. He had volunteered despite being a married man with four little girls, aged between 7 and 2 years old.

That day, 500 Liverpool Pals were killed, leaving the whole city and region to grieve. The nature of the constitution of the Pals meant that, when there was a large loss of soldiers, few people could fail to know at least one of the fallen.

By July 1916, the time of the Somme offensive, there had been 420,000 British soldiers killed, which was more than twice the number of the entire army in 1914.

Besides the horrific experience of fighting, losing comrades and living with constant fear, battened down in order to do one's duty, there were other hardships. It was intended that soldiers should not go hungry and, certainly, no soldier starved, but the logistics of distributing food supplies meant that often the diet was not tasty or nutritious. A repetitive menu at the front lines of bully beef (corned beef) and hard tack biscuits meant that many men suffered from digestive problems. Another detested regular was Maconochie, named after the company in Aberdeen that manufactured this tinned mixture of fatty meat and vegetables in thin gravy. Most men only ate it because they were hungry. The biscuits were made by Huntley & Palmer, then the biggest biscuit producer in the country. They were made from flour, salt and water, and were so hard that the troops likened them to dog biscuits and dipped them in tea or even plain water in order to make it possible to bite them.

When supplies were coming through, soldiers would also have jam, sugar, cheese and condensed milk. Sometimes they would receive a supply of bacon. They had to be careful not to create smoke in cooking bacon, because this would attract German shellfire.

Tea was vital to the troops. It was familiar and comforting and helped to disguise the sometimes tainted water, which might have been transported in petrol cans. Flour became difficult to obtain, so bread was adulterated with dried potatoes, barley, oats and even pulverised straw.

It is easy to understand the welcome that parcels from home received. These might contain chocolate or trench cake, from a recipe that meant the cake would keep well. Wives and mothers who made this cake would surely have adjusted the recipe to what was available, especially as rationing made various things scarce or unobtainable. But it would still have been good for the digestion to have some dried fruit, and good for morale to have a taste of home, baked with love.

Men who were based at the same location for some time grew vegetables, went fishing, poached game and bought food from the locals. Impromptu cafés, known as *estaminets*, sprang up and those who ran them soon learned that the soldiers did not admire their cuisine. Consequently, they often served large plates of egg and chips, washed down by *vin blanc*, or 'plonk' as it came to be known.

As well as many thousands of men serving at the front, there were animals which were vitally necessary to the war effort. Lord Lathom had granted permission, through his trustees, for the War Department to use Lathom Park, near Ormskirk, without charge for the training of men and horses, so thousands of men and horses were trained there. Horses were brought from other parts of Britain, but also, through Liverpool's Canada Dock, horses and mules were imported

TRENCH CAKE
8oz plain flour
2 teaspoons cocoa
4oz margarine
½ teaspoon baking soda
1 teaspoon vinegar
¼ pint milk
3oz brown sugar
3oz currants
Nutmeg, ginger, lemon rind

Grease tin. Rub margarine into flour. Add dry ingredients. Mix well. Add baking soda dissolved in the vinegar and milk. Beat well. Turn into tin. Bake in a moderate oven for about two hours.

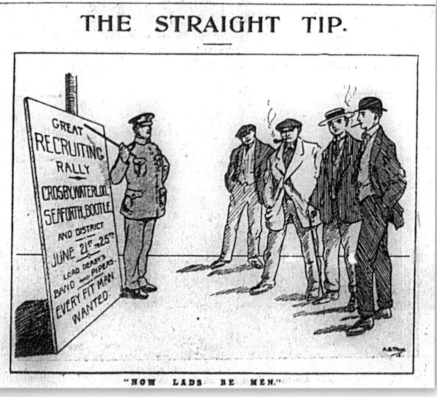

THE STRAIGHT TIP.

GREAT RECRUITING RALLY
CROSBY,WATERLOO, SEAFORTH, BOOTLE
AND DISTRICT
JUNE 21ST TO 25TH
LORD DERBY'S BAND AND PIPERS
EVERY FIT MAN WANTED.

"NOW LADS BE MEN."

The Straight Tip':
an appeal to manly
pride.

from Ireland, South Africa and South America and transferred by train to Ormskirk railway station and then to Lathom Park, which had its own station.

Many more horses, and also mules, were used for work such as pulling gun carriages and carrying ammunition and other important supplies to the front, than were used as cavalry horses. Many horses died because of the sometimes dreadful weather and appalling conditions, including the mud, which made such heavy work much worse. It is difficult to be sure how many horses were trained at Lathom, but between August and November 1914 more than 215,000 had been brought there. Thousands of men came to Lathom to learn equine skills, and others came as already skilled farriers and blacksmiths who were still civilians. But when the park became a military estate in 1915, these men also, suddenly, became soldiers. It was cheaper for the authorities to pay soldiers than to employ private labour.

Meanwhile, at sea, Liverpool men were also serving their country.

The Royal Navy was one of the largest and, arguably, best trained in the world. It gave the nation a feeling of security to be protected by such a powerful fleet. There had been one shock attack in December 1914, when the coastal towns of Whitby, Hartlepool and Scarborough had been shelled by German cruisers. However, when a further surprise attack was attempted a month later, the Germans were intercepted by British ships, which sank the cruiser *Blücher*. Discouraged, there was very little activity by the *Kaiserliche Marine* (German Navy) for more than a year.

G. R.
BLACKSMITHS.

Blacksmiths are urgently required for service in the Royal Engineers, for the duration of the War. Men desiring to enlist as Blacksmiths in the Royal Engineers are put through a test at their trade which is less difficult than the test for Shoeing Smiths; they might for example be required to cut off a length from ¼ inch sound bar iron, bend into ring of 5 inches diameter, and weld complete.

For terms of Pay and Service apply to

RECRUITING OFFICE, TOWN HALL, SOUTHPORT.

GOD SAVE THE KING.

Blacksmiths asked to enlist in the Royal Engineers.

The battle fought from 31 May to 1 June 1916 in the North Sea became known as the Battle of Jutland because it was fought near the coast of Denmark's Jutland Peninsula. It was the largest naval battle and the only full-scale clash of battleships in the war. The intention of Germany's High Seas Fleet was to lure out, trap and destroy a portion of the Grand Fleet – the main part of the fleet of the British Navy, formed by Admiral Jellicoe – because the German naval force was not great enough to engage the entire British fleet. In essence, the Germans wanted to break the blockade of Germany, while the British aim was to contain the German Navy and, thus, keep Britain's shipping lanes clear.

Fourteen British and eleven German ships were sunk, with great loss of life. Both sides claimed victory. The British lost more ships and twice as many sailors but succeeded in containing the German fleet. The Germans turned to submarine warfare and it was the resultant destruction of Allied and neutral shipping which, by April 1917, was one of the causes of the United States' declaration of war on Germany.

Prince Albert, the second son of George V, was a young midshipman aboard HMS *Collingwood*, during this battle. Fortunately, he survived to become George VI in 1936. He is the only British sovereign to have seen genuine active service since William IV.

A maritime city such as Liverpool was sure to have many men of all ranks serving in the Royal Navy and this is reflected in the number of Merseyside casualties at the Battle of Jutland; the *Liverpool Echo*, over the days and weeks after the battle, lists over 150 names of men and boys lost at Jutland. There were grim columns of names, each one a tragic loss to their families and to the city. This number also reflects only the names of those men of whom the paper was aware, and therefore the number of those lost was almost certainly greater than those listed.

Among the names is that of Lieutenant Richard Eadson Paterson, aged 22, 'the dearly loved younger son of Professor and Mrs A.M. Paterson of 21, Abercromby Square, Liverpool'.

Abercromby Square is at the heart of the buildings of the University of Liverpool. It was also the home of the Chavasse family. Richard's father, Andrew Melville Paterson CBE, had a distinguished medical and academic career. He and his wife had five children and it was their youngest son, who had pursued a naval career from the age of 12, who was killed at the Battle of Jutland.

Some of the messages *in memoriam* include some biographical details of the fallen, even though most of them were so young that they had only brief lives to relate. Corporal Richard Ellis Shaw, for instance, was in the Royal Marines: 'a native of Formby, he was on HMS *Black Prince*, although only 23 years old, he had seen nearly eight years service. He was aboard HMS *Cochrane* when she escorted the King to India for the Coronation Durbar. His brother, Lawrence, is a Private in the 7th KLR.'

An even younger casualty of the Battle of Jutland was Albert George England; he was born in 1898 and had not reached his 18th birthday when he was killed. He is described in the *Liverpool Echo* as 'a rating boy on HMS *Defence*. He joined the Navy in March 1914. He lived with his parents at 21, Walton Lane. He was home on leave just three weeks before the battle. He attended Boundary Street East Primitive Methodist Church all his life.'

This church's memorial records all forty-one names of its members who served in the Great War, of whom only four were killed, including Albert England and Arthur Jackson, killed on the Somme. Albert is also recorded on the Plymouth Naval Memorial.

Two brothers were killed on 31 May 1916. The *Liverpool Echo* records that they were 'killed in a great sea battle at Jutland. Private Albert Victor Stephenson, RMLI, aged 24, on HMS *Defence* and Gunner Garton Grey Stephenson, RMA, aged 20, on HMS *Indefatigable*, two beloved and affectionate sons of Corporal William Stephenson, RFA, serving in France and Mrs Stephenson of 32, Second Avenue, Fazakerley. In honour's cause.'

It is impossible to encompass the grief and loneliness of Mrs Stephenson in the loss of two sons and the continuing anxiety about her husband, still in danger every day. Families were well aware that when they received reassuring letters from their loved ones, during the lapse of time between writing and receipt of the news, the situation could have changed.

Shipping was in constant danger from the activities of U-boats, threatening the ships, trade and lives. John Ferguson McWhor was a Mersey pilot during the First World War, attached to the White Star line, and piloted many ships that were bound for New York. In November 1916, there was an occasion when it was deemed unsafe for John to leave the ship at the Mersey Bar or at Point Lynas, off Anglesey. His wife was astonished to receive a telegram from him reporting his safe arrival in New York. John is recorded as a passenger aboard the *St Paul*, arriving at Liverpool on his return from his enforced journey to New York.

The United States entered the war on 6 April 1917. A strong contributing factor to this change of heart from the country's original neutrality was the activity of the U-boats. The worsening situation had been reinforced by the public outrage caused in the States by the earlier loss of American civilian lives aboard the *Lusitania*.

The first American arrival in Liverpool on 18 May 1917 was a hospital unit of Harvard University students, who were welcomed by the American consul and a British general. Before their journey to France, the students were temporarily billeted in Blackpool.

Commander-in-chief of the American Expeditionary Force (AEF) was General John Joseph Pershing. He arrived aboard the RMS *Baltic* at Liverpool on 8 June 1917 and remained in the city for four days before moving on to France.

The Cunard line's SS *Saxonia* was used from September 1917 to transport American troops between New York and Liverpool, which was the busiest port in the country with nearly 8,500 troops and nurses arriving between May 1917 and the end of the war.

Some American troops were actually billeted in the Liverpool area. There was a large American army camp at Knotty Ash, originally comprising tents but later including wooden huts. Regular entertainment was laid on at the camp, and soldiers stationed there enjoyed entry to Picton Road Public Baths.

The YMCA set up a 'hut' in Lord Street in February 1918, but this was so well appointed that it was more like a hotel with a games room, lounge, canteen and beds for forty men. It was managed by Americans, but staffed by women volunteers. It was so well used that a larger premises was soon opened. This was Lincoln Lodge in School Lane.

EVERTON FOOTBALL CLUB

There were baseball games for the American troops at Knotty Ash and an exhibition game, featuring the New York Giants and the Chicago White Sox, at Goodison Park. There was also an American Football game at the ground, which, earlier in the war, had been used by the Territorial Army for drill practice.

Other facilities were provided by the American Red Cross; there were canteens and supplies available in all the camps in Great Britain. One of its three large supply warehouses was in Liverpool.

On 31 May 1918 the largest convoy, about 33,000 American troops, arrived in Liverpool. A meeting was held on 14 June 1918 at Liverpool Town Hall to consider how to welcome and cope with the large numbers of American troops who would pass through Liverpool – the gateway to the world or, certainly, to the United States! The mayors of Wallasey, Bootle and Birkenhead, as well as the mayor of Liverpool, attended. They had also to consider troops who were on leave in England and those who were billeted locally.

Liverpool began to celebrate American public holidays. Independence Day in July was celebrated at St George's Plateau with many American troops who had marched in from Knotty Ash to the city centre; bands played appropriate music and the mayor gave a speech. There was a dinner dance at Port Sunlight after a day of sports, including a baseball game.

In November, Thanksgiving was celebrated with a dinner dance at Birkenhead Town Hall for 250 American sailors. A corresponding number of respectable young women were invited. The Town Hall was decorated with flags and flowers and a buffet was provided. New Brighton Tower ballroom was also a venue for weekly dances and, in Liverpool, a service of Thanksgiving was held at the Knotty Ash camp as well as a programme of sports throughout the day.

In addition to these public events, American soldiers were welcomed into people's homes. One such scheme was arranged by the Liverpool Rotary Club, whereby local families threw their homes open for a week to an American soldier who was on leave. About 300 homes in the Liverpool area were involved in this scheme by June 1918.

Independence Day, 1918, celebrated on St George's Plateau.

Just as Liverpool had an important part to play in bringing these troops into the country, billeting them and sending them on to their destinations, so the city had a responsibility for sending thousands of soldiers on their journey home.

The camp at Knotty Ash again played an important part in processing soldiers waiting to return to New York. The railway stations, especially Lime Street station, were crowded with Americans who had travelled to Liverpool to try to engage a passage on one of the liners at the landing stage. The great port was busy with liners setting off on their voyages across the Atlantic to take our allies home.

5

WHILE YOU'RE AWAY

The conduct of war on the home front is critical for victory. Wars are known to be won and lost on the home front. The Great War was arguably the first war where the part played by those at home was absolutely crucial.

There had been an enormous impact on the lives of civilians from the very beginning of the war. There had been a huge drive to recruitment, including a poster campaign using a number of techniques to persuade men to enlist. When the direct appeal of Kitchener's famous statement 'Your country needs you' – the most successful poster used during the war – did not produce sufficient numbers for the insatiable war machine, a poster proclaiming that 'Women of Britain say Go!' suggested to men that their wives and sweethearts wanted them to fight. The poster was intended to appeal to the chivalric urge to defend one's womenfolk. There was even a poster implying that if mothers did not want their sons to fight, there was something wrong with the way in which their sons had been brought up. Another poster was aimed at family men; the authorities were concerned that fathers may have been less willing to go to war than young lads, filled with the spirit of adventure. This poster showed children posing the question, 'Daddy, what did you do in the Great War?' There were also posters suggesting that young women ought not to 'keep company' with men who had not volunteered. These posters were not just aimed at recruiting men to fight, but also at influencing people's attitudes to the war.

Patriotic sentiments in the 'Comrades' Marching Song'.

When still more men were required, the government introduced conscription. From March 1916, military service became compulsory for all single men in England, Scotland and Wales aged 18 to 41, except those who were in jobs essential to the war effort, the sole support of dependants, medically unfit, or 'those who could show a conscientious objection'. This latter clause was a significant inclusion that was intended to defuse opposition to conscription. Further military service laws included married men, tightened occupational exemptions and raised the age limit to 50. Perhaps because of the real need for men to join the army, conscientious objectors (COs) could be imprisoned and lasting social stigma was attached to this category. Many of those who applied for exemption on other grounds were refused.

There were approximately 16,000 British men on record as COs to armed service during the First World War. This figure does not include men who may have had anti-war sentiments but were unfit, in reserved occupations, or had felt peer group pressure to join the forces, regardless of their private thoughts. The number of COs may appear small compared with the 6 million men who served, but the impact of these men on public opinion and on future governments was to have lasting effects.

There were four main reasons why men objected to armed service during the Great War. The best known was an objection to violence and killing for religious reasons. For instance, pacifism was a crucial belief for the Society of Friends, known as Quakers; but because some Quaker men did enlist, the general public were not convinced of the sincerity of those who used this argument to refuse to fight. Then there were Christian fundamentalists, who took the Bible literally and quoted 'Thou shalt not kill'. There were also people who believed that killing was intrinsically wrong, but not on religious grounds.

A smaller group were those who objected on political grounds. This group included some members of the Socialist Labour Party, who saw the war as an imperialist war; they believed that it had been brought about by the ruling classes but had been left to the workers to fight. This group ignored the fact that many of the young men and women who were enlisted in the services or involved in nursing and other activities supporting the waging of war were not from working-class backgrounds. There was a strong suspicion among the general public that all these reasons were, in fact, excuses.

Conscientious objectors took different stances on participation in the war effort. The absolutists refused any work which could be seen as supporting the war effort, which could extend

The Hefty Shirker seeks to shelter behind others.

‑EVENING EXPRESS. LIVERPOOL. WEDNES

WILL HE BE FETCHED?

Hefty Shirker: "Recruiting success even better than expected." That puts me safe.

[Men who have enlisted under the Derby system now want to know what the Government will do to bring into line the shirkers who are trusting to the success of the scheme to save them from military service.]

to almost any activity that kept the country running. Then there were the alternativists, who were willing to work in occupations not controlled by the army. A third group accepted military service in a non-combatant role; many of these men served in the Royal Army Medical Corps (RAMC) as medics or front-line stretcher bearers. At times, they were in as much danger as those who were fighting.

Over 3,000 conscientious objectors joined the Non-Combatant Corps (NCC), dubbed the No-Courage Corps by the press. It was set up in March 1916 as part of the army and was run by regular army officers. The COs assigned to it were army privates, who wore army uniforms and were subject to army discipline, but did not carry weapons or take part in battle. Their duties were mainly to provide cleaning, building, and loading and unloading anything except munitions, in support of the military. Some of the COs were concerned that the activities of the NCC members released another man to fight and die in their places. But refusing any involvement at all would not save lives in any case; it was an insoluble dilemma.

In 1914, a group of Quakers were trained in first aid, and began the Friends Ambulance Unit (FAU) in France. Most of its 1,200 members were pacifists; they were all civilians but they worked beside the fighting soldiers. The FAU provided its COs with a way to support the wounded but not the war.

There is no doubt that the fate of conscientious objectors varied greatly. Neither the government nor the army had any experience of military conscription, let alone the issues raised by those who refused to serve.

When these men were able to be used in alternative schemes, such as the FAU, this was often seen as an accept-able solution to the problem. On the other hand, those who refused to countenance any form of service which might be construed as supporting the war could be sent to prison. Some were sentenced to as long as ten years' penal servitude and those who were sentenced to remain in prison for the duration of the war were not released until all the serving soldiers had returned home. Some were not released until August 1919. Nearly 6,500 COs were court-martialled and sent to prison, where they, like other prisoners at the time, undertook hard labour, suffered the 'no talking' rule and sometimes received a bread and water diet.

From 1916, when conscription was introduced, until 1919, which was after the armistice, Walton Gaol housed a number of conscientious objectors.

The greater number of the general public, at that time, were not sympathetic – their husbands, brothers and sons were involved in the war. Indeed, by the time that conscription was introduced, many people had lost family members, sweethearts or friends. They asked, why should these men expect to be treated differently?

Charitable events and activities were a large part of daily life during the war for those at home and there were many worthy causes that needed support. Early in the war, efforts to help the Belgian refugees had been predominant, but as the war progressed and lengthened, the focus of people's attention altered.

Nearly 18,000 charities were begun during the war years. Naturally, at the forefront of these were 'comforts for the troops'. This description included food, such as trench cake, books and clothing sent to British and Empire troops. There were also charities that aimed to provide medical services and support for disabled servicemen.

Flag Days were part of daily life: people contributed generously.

The British Red Cross in Liverpool sent out many tons of basic food supplies as well as thousands of articles of second-hand clothing to prisoners in Germany and to prisoners of war in England.

There were also organisations that were intent on relieving distress at home. When conscription began, the loss of the main breadwinner or, in some cases, father and sons who had been contributing to the household fund, meant considerable hardship for some families, especially where the presence of younger children meant that the mother was unable to look for employment herself. The government had realised men would

People were encouraged to contribute to War Loans and Bonds.

not volunteer to fight if they did not believe that their homes and families would be looked after. Conscription had meant that they had no choice, but charitable effort was intended to go some way to alleviate need for the family and anxiety for the servicemen.

Among the most popular causes were tobacco and cigarettes for the troops and one of the largest charities was the Smokes for Wounded Soldiers and Sailors Society, which was known popularly as the SSS. The charity held 'Fag Days' rather than Flag Days and raised sufficient funds to be able to distribute vast quantities of 'smokes' in cigarettes and tobacco to wounded men. One estimate is that more than a billion cigarettes were donated by this charity.

In Liverpool, St George's Hall and the impressive plateau in front of it had been central to the enlisting of the Pals regiments, and the hall itself had been the venue for the medicals that followed recruitment. After the soldiers had gone to war, the plateau became the focal point for many fundraising events. Liverpool people were encouraged to buy War Bonds: propaganda posters now appeared showing a small girl asking her father to buy her some. Aeroplanes and tanks would be displayed and generous sums of money were raised as a result.

In fact, for most of the population, fundraising became a routine part of life in wartime. Liverpool, although many of its people were not rich, was an open-hearted and generous community and, since many thousands of Liverpool men were now serving in some capacity, these causes were very close to home.

Entertainment at Sun Hall, Stanley Road, Bootle.

SUN HALL,

STANLEY ROAD, BOOTLE,

Proprietor and Licensee—J. LESLIE GREENE.

Week Commencing APRIL 19th.

MONDAY, TUESDAY, and WEDNESDAY,

Exclusive Exhibition to this Theatre, the Great Patriotic Drama,

Call of the Motherland,

A Thrilling and Intensely Impressive War Drama founded upon dramatic incidents in the present conflict, with a powerful and exciting plot. War scenes and encounters, and thrilling combats abound in the course of the story, which rivet the attention of the spectators from start to finish.

THURSDAY, FRIDAY, and SATURDAY,

Exclusive to this Theatre, and first time of exhibition,

Sexton Blake,

AND THE STOLEN HEIRLOOMS,

A Thrilling Detective Romance, in which this sagacious investigator is one too many for the criminals.

NEXT WEEK.

STARRING ENGAGEMENT.

For Three Nights only, and Monday and Wednesday Matinees,

In consequence of innumerable requests, Welcome Return Visit of the World's Sweetheart,

Miss Mary Pickford

In her Greatest Success,

"BEHIND THE SCENES."

Hundreds were unable to obtain admission on the last occasion.

GRAND ORCHESTRA.

Every Evening at 8. Matinees MONDAYS, WEDNESDAYS, and SATURDAYS at 3.

POPULAR PRICES.

Local newspapers carried details of forthcoming dances, bazaars, fetes and sales of produce and work. Most women spent a good deal of their leisure hours in knitting or other handiwork. In one sense this may have been a displacement activity, a feeling of 'doing something', an attempt to distract oneself from ever-present anxiety for their menfolk. Later issues of the newspapers would give details of the money raised and goods collected at these events. In the streets of Liverpool and the surrounding area, posters advertised wartime charities, and women carried trays bearing lapel-pin flags, or picture postcards to be sold for various causes.

There was some opposition to certain charities. Queen Mary's Needlework Guild was opposed by the War Emergency Workers' National Committee, predominantly a Labour group, which was

The prestigious Henderson's Store Roll of Honour.

Children involved in fundraising enjoy a party at Liverpool Town Hall.

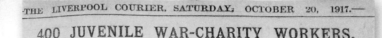

THE LIVERPOOL COURIER, SATURDAY, OCTOBER 20, 1917.—

400 JUVENILE WAR-CHARITY WORKERS.

COURIER PHOTO.

Yesterday afternoon, at the Town Hall, over 400 Liverpool school children were entertained in recognition of their work for the various war charities of the city. The photograph shows some of them in the large ballroom enjoying the ever-fresh drama of Punch and Judy.

THE GREAT WAR PRIZE CERTIFICATE

During the war, children were asked to sacrifice any prizes that they might merit and accept a Prize Certificate instead. The signature on these certificates was that of James W. Alsop, chairman of the Liverpool Education Committee. I have one of these certificates awarded to my father, Alfred Brown of Heyworth Street School.

concerned that women in the textile and clothing industry, already finding their jobs threatened by the loss of export markets resulting from the war, now perceived another threat from the guild.

As a result, the queen created the Queen's Work for Women Fund. Contracts to supply clothing and other items for the Army Supply Department were issued and the queen placed a personal order for 75,000 woollen body belts as part of her Christmas gift to the troops.

Children were also encouraged to play an active part in the war effort by donating their breakfasts to Egg Day, on which eggs were collected for wounded soldiers. Small children were frequently used in fundraising, dressed as soldiers and nurses.

There was concern about animals involved in war work, which prompted the formation or expansion of several welfare organisations. The Blue Cross Fund aimed to be the equivalent for animals of the Red Cross and became known especially for its work with horses. At first, the War Office saw this as unnecessary, but the fund soon established horse hospitals and provided treatments, equipment, vets and ambulances in battlefield areas. Contributions from the public were generous for the war work of the Blue Cross.

The information that the general public received about the progress and events of the war was sporadic. Almost everyone was waiting for news of their loved ones from the front, from those at sea or from those who were serving behind the lines, such as nurses, who were not necessarily safe from danger.

Children played their part in the war economy.

Empire Day at Arnot Street School, Walton.

WALTER HEWITT
Walter Hewitt was the first engineer aboard the MV *Rhineland* which was mined and sunk in the North Sea. Twenty-one lives besides Walter's were lost, including the captain. Walter was the son of William and Annie Hewitt and lived at 12, Grace Road, Aintree.

Newspapers were censored, as were soldiers' letters home. When a man was killed, his officer might write to his family minimising the reality of what had happened to him. It is difficult to know how far these letters with their comforting 'white lies' were believed, since this must have depended on the nature of the recipient.

Some attempts to influence people's thinking were unpredictable in their results. For instance, in 1916, a film entitled *The Somme* was an attempt to encourage support for the troops, but it was too graphic for most people to bear and extremely upsetting to see men killed in action

A German Naval Victory

" With joyful pride we contemplate this latest deed of our navy."
Kölnische Volkszeitung, 10th May, 1915.

This medal has been struck in Germany with the object of keeping alive in German hearts the recollection of the glorious achievement of the German Navy in deliberately destroying an unarmed passenger ship, together with 1,198 non-combatants, men, women and children.

On the obverse, under the legend "No contraband" *(Keine Bannware),* there is a representation of the *Lusitania* sinking. The designer has put in guns and aeroplanes, which (as was certified by United States Government officials after inspection) the *Lusitania* did *not* carry ; but has conveniently omitted to put in the women and children, which the world knows she did carry.

On the reverse, under the legend "Business above all" *(Geschäft über alles),* the figure of Death sits at the booking office of the Cunard Line and gives out tickets to passengers, who refuse to attend to the warning against submarines given by a German. This picture seeks apparently to propound the theory that if a murderer warns his victim of his intention, the guilt of the crime will rest with the victim, not with the murderer.

A German naval victory: sinking the Lusitania.

on screen, especially when so many people had men serving in the army in France. About a million people saw the film at their local cinema in the first six weeks after it was released.

There was concern in the government that morale at home should be high. But some events could not be concealed. There were Zeppelin raids after 1915 with civilian casualties and, although the range of the bombers was limited, there was general anxiety about the possibility of being bombed.

One event that caused widespread outrage was the sinking of RMS *Lusitania* in 1915. This was a major event of the Great War. Many historians have agreed that it was an important factor leading to the Americans joining the combat.

RMS *Lusitania* is regarded as the second most famous ship to be lost at sea, after the *Titanic*, because she was a special liner. Launched in 1906, she had been the world's largest passenger

THE LIVERPOOL COURIER. TUESDAY. MARCH 30. 1915.

OVER YOU GO!

In their piratical career the Germans are sacrificing men, women, and children.

This cartoon appeared before the sinking of the Lusitania.

ship until the Cunard line also launched the *Mauretania*. *Lusitania* was a holder of the Blue Riband and already familiar to the Germans, who were fierce competitors in the transatlantic trade. The *Lusitania* and *Mauretania* were luxury ships, which had lifts and electric light; they had much more passenger space than other ships, and the first-class decks were particularly remarkable for their comfort and style.

In May 1915, when *Lusitania* crossed the Atlantic Ocean, aggressive German submarine warfare was at its height. Germany saw the seas around the British Isles as a war zone. When the *Lusitania* was 11 miles from the southern coast of Ireland, she was torpedoed. There was a second explosion some moments after the torpedo struck its target and the ship sank with a loss of 1,198 lives, including 785 passengers and 413 crew members; among this number there were 128 citizens of the United States. There was public outrage in the States, and in Britain, at this attack on a non-naval vessel. The German embassy in the United States had issued a warning in fifty newspapers that any ship flying British colours was a legitimate target. The Germans were accused of breaching international laws, while German justification for attacking the *Lusitania* was that the ship was carrying hundreds of tons of war munitions, therefore making it a legitimate military target. This was widely dismissed as German propaganda, although the second, unexplained explosion does suggest that there might have been some truth in the claim.

Lusitania's chief engineer, Bryce of Crosby.

The effects of the loss of the *Lusitania* were felt immediately in Liverpool. Many of the crew came from the city, and especially from its northern end, where many families of Irish origin were interrelated and mutually dependent. It was a catastrophe for this district, with its networks of small houses, that so many of its menfolk were lost. The economic effects on this community would be

CHIEF ENGINEER BRYCE, OF CROSBY.

Mr. Archibald Bryce, the chief engineer who is among the lost, resided at College-road, Great Crosby. He joined the Cunard service in 1884, as a junior engineer on the s.s. Cephalonia, and has served on a large number of the steamers of the fleet, including the Tarifa, Trinidad, and Saragossa in the Mediterranean trade; Scythia, Bothnia, Aurania, Etruria, Campania, Caronia, Carmania, Mauretania, and Lusitania in the Atlantic service. The Carmania was Mr. Bryce's first turbine steamer. He became second engineer of her in November, 1905, and in September of the following year he was appointed second second. In November, 1911, he became intermediate second engineer of the Mauretania, and in December, the same year, was appointed senior second of the same steamship. In January, 1913, he was transferred to the Lusitania as senior second, and in July, last year, was promoted to be chief engineer. Later he became chief engineer of the Aquitania, but following closely the experience of Captain Turner, he recently returned to the Lusitania.

Mr. Bryce's father was also a Cunard engineer, commencing in 1848, on the company's paddle steamers, and ending, in 1886, as chief engineer of the Gallia.

Anti-German cartoon after the sinking of the Lusitania.

felt for many decades after the event, just as whole communities were decimated by the Pals system of recruitment.

Among the many men from this area of the city who were lost on the *Lusitania* on 7 May 1915 was Fireman John Kelly, aged 36, of 53, Lathom Street, Kirkdale, the son of Margaret and the late John Kelly. John is recorded on the memorial at St Alphonsus Roman Catholic (RC) church, Kirkdale.

Leading Fireman John James Burns, aged 48, appears on the same memorial and also on the memorial at St James RC Church, Bootle, since he had lived in both parishes. John was the son of John, born in Dublin, and Margaret, born in Limerick. He married Janet Dickson and was last residing at 13, York Street, Bootle with his wife and their four children, William John, Mary Winnefred, Francis Anthony and Joseph James, together with Janet's mother, Mary Dickson.

Also lost on the *Lusitania* were father and son, Fireman Michael Cooney and Fireman Michael Cooney, aged 20. Both men appear on the memorial in St Anthony's RC Church, Scotland Road, Liverpool. They lived at 92, Hopwood Street, Liverpool. There is some doubt about the age of Michael (senior) who appears on the memorial records as 40 years old in 1915, but as 46 years old on the 1911 census. It may be that, like so many, he reduced his age in order to serve, since his employment is recorded as an 'assistant' in 1911, not as a seaman.

Following the loss of the *Lusitania* with so many Liverpool men, riots broke out in the city and spread through the rest of the country. It has been suggested that these riots originated with the families of the dead sailors, but there is no evidence to support this claim. At the end of the rioting and looting, none of those charged with damage or looting had a relative serving on the ship.

UNDYING FAME FOR THE 7th.

The following letters from Drummer Alfred Orme and Private Lawrence Orme have been received by their parents, Mr. and Mrs. David Orme, 7, South-road, Waterloo:—

Drummer Orme writes:—I know only too well how anxious you will have been this last few days about Lawrence and myself. Well, God has most surely answered your prayers, for Lawrence and myself are quite safe. How we both managed to escape I don't know; this last few days has been perfect hell on earth. Our lads have behaved fine. We have lost a lot of fine chaps, but they went to their death like men, and have made undying fame for the good old 7th Liverpools. Our company has lost all its officers, including Major Hughes. Although it is not fair to single anybody out, I think our Major deserves special mention. His one cry in the charge was "Remember the Lusitania." We captured all the German trenches and got the Germans on the open country, and even when we had captured the last German trench our Major went out throwing bombs at the pigs, but he never came back. He met his death "Remembering the Lusitania." My own

Remembering the Lusitania: others were inspired by the event.

One man who was brought before the judge at Dale Street said that he had served aboard the *Lusitania* a few months earlier and was motivated by revenge for the attack on his ship. It was shown that he had never served aboard the ship and was using the sinking to justify his crimes.

Shops were attacked on County Road, Walton Lane and Fountains Road. As the attacks progressed, the crowds grew and about sixty police officers were struggling to contain them. In Robson Street, a pork butcher's shop was attacked and nineteen arrests were made.

The disturbances continued on the following day. Dimler's shop in County Road was again attacked and there was further trouble in Fox Street, Juvenal Street, Mile End, Heyworth Street and Richmond Row. A pork butcher's shop on Scotland Road was damaged and all of its contents were stolen. An underlying motive for this lawlessness may have been anger about the difficulty of feeding a family with reduced food supplies and, at this time, no proper system of rationing. Yet there were many poor, but proud and respectable, people who did not become involved in these illegal acts.

Violence accompanied all these attacks and public houses across Liverpool were obliged to close their doors by 6 p.m. There were sixty-seven arrests by the end of that weekend.

This is a sad episode in the history of Liverpool. By Monday, it was clear

IMPORTANT NOTICE.

THE ENGLISH PORK BUTCHER'S SHOPS

216 Marsh Lane and 173 Linacre Rd.,

in the occupation of

GEO. BOWRING

will re-open at the earliest possible moment after damage has been repaired. I wish to express my thanks to my many customers for past favours, and trust to be supported by their patronage in the future.

All English. No Germans Employed.

I remain,

yours faithfully,

GEO. BOWRING.

Top: George Bowring advertises his English pork butcher's shop.

AT LITHERLAND.

FORTY CASES AT COUNTY MAGIS-TRATES' COURT.

Over forty persons were brought before the Liverpool County Magistrates at the Sessions Court, Islington, on Tuesday morning, charged with looting.

The majority of the offenders were women, and a few were young girls.

Supt. Wilcock said three shops in Linacre-road were smashed in and looted by the riotous crowd. Two of them were known as the Crown Stores, and were kept by Frederich William Hassaghen, a chandler. The other shop, 173, Linacre-road, was in the occupation of George E. Bowring, a pork butcher.

Both the prosecutors, the superintendent continued, were British subjects, Hassaghen having been born in Liverpool. The attacks on the shops commenced about nine o'clock at night, and went on until midnight. A large crowd collected, and after throwing stones through the windows entered the premises and commenced looting on an extensive scale, taking away crockery, food, furniture, clothing—everything they could lay their hands on, in fact.

Bottom: Litherland magistrates: report of looting and sentencing.

LIVERPOOL FOOTBALL CLUB

Liverpool competed in a regional league – the Lancashire Section – during the war. They won several trophies. Liverpool players fought in the war, including Philip Bratley, Robert Crawford and Wilfred Bartrop, who was the only one to be killed. He died in the last struggle on 7 November 1918, fighting in Belgium.

that children as well as adults were taking violent action against any shop that appeared to be owned by Germans. The trouble moved to the south end of the city and the crowds grew. At one time, it was estimated that 2,000 people were involved and shops in Upper Hill Street, North Hill Street, Mill Street, Lodge Lane, Northumberland Street, Warwick Street, St James Street and Crown Street were attacked.

At its worst, as the looting and violence increased and spread, the police were struggling to control the problem and the chief constable of Liverpool asked the Home Office for help from the military. This was agreed but the troops were never actually brought onto the streets.

Those found guilty at the magistrates' court in Dale Street were, initially, dealt with by being remanded for seven days. However, the judge pointed out that the fate of the *Lusitania* was not a justification for lawless behaviour and warned that any future offences would be dealt with more severely.

When a further forty-five people were sentenced to prison for between twenty-one and twenty-eight days, it was clear that the judge had meant what he said; furthermore, the judge pointed out that a number of men involved appeared of military age and suggested that if they wanted to fight the Germans then they should do it in a military uniform. This seems to be a just summing-up of the situation.

Some of the great Liverpool events were suspended during the war years.

The Grand National, run on 28 March 1919, was the first since 1915. It was won by jockey Ernest (Ernie) Piggott, riding Poethlyn. This pair had won an unofficial Grand National run at Gatwick Racecourse in 1918. Ernie won the Grand National three times; his son was also a successful jockey and his grandson, Lester Piggott, was British Flat Race Champion Jockey eleven times.

Football had continued into 1915 because there was a belief on some sides that 'the war would be over by Christmas' and, also, that football matches would help to maintain good morale among the public. Everton had won the First Division Championship in the 1914/15 season and Liverpool had reached the Cup Final. But competitive football was suspended after 1915.

An Athletes Volunteer Force was set up and Liverpool and Everton players commenced drill on 29 September 1914. There were also rifle ranges set up at Goodison Park and Anfield and the two teams jointly engaged an instructor for both drill and rifle practice. Practices took place alternately at the two grounds on Tuesday, Wednesday and Thursday at 3.30 p.m. each day.

Liverpool was a city with many theatres and music halls throughout the war, but, particularly at the beginning, the theatre was used to recruit men to the army. Vesta Tilley, the male impersonator, was at the forefront of this type of entertainment and was known as 'Britain's best recruiting sergeant' since men were asked to join the army on stage during her shows. The heightened emotion and peer group pressure of the moment made many enthusiastic young men 'take the shilling'. Vesta was known to come among the audience and place her hand on a man's shoulder to urge him forward.

There were many songs that captured the spirit of different periods of the war. Some of them, like 'Goodbye, Dolly Grey' were already being sung in the Boer War. Others were more recent: the well-known 'It's a Long Way to Tipperary' was written by Jack Judge and Henry Williams in 1912. At the beginning of the war, the songs sung by the troops reflected their optimistic attitude. Many of them truly believed that the war would be over quickly and that this was their opportunity to show their patriotism and have an adventure away from home.

In 1915, Felix and George wrote 'Pack Up Your Troubles in Your Old Kit Bag and Smile, Smile, Smile', the tone of which was still remarkably cheerful. However, as the war progressed and conscription was introduced the mood began to change. Bennett Scott, a well-known writer of music hall songs such as 'Ship Ahoy', wrote 'Take Me Back to Dear Old Blighty' with co-writers Fred Godfrey and A.J. Mills. This song reflected the mood of the men in the trenches, which was very different after the mind-numbingly high numbers of casualties and everyday general discomforts, such as being perpetually wet and cold, and ridden with vermin, to which they were subjected.

Ivor Novello's 'Keep the Home Fires Burning' was intended to reinforce the fortitude of those on the home front. It was originally called 'Till the Boys Come Home'.

Harry Lauder, an enormously popular music hall star, was also a writer of some of his own material. His only son, Captain John Lauder, of the 8th Battalion of the Argyll and Sutherland Highlanders, was killed on 28 December 1916 at Poiziers. Harry wrote the song 'Keep Right On to the End of the Road' after John's death. This song remains popular and the chorus captures the feelings of stoicism, sacrifice and longing for eventual reunion that must have been universally experienced during the Great War:

> Keep right on to the end of the road
> Keep right on to the end
> Tho' the way be long, let your heart be strong
> Keep right on to the end
> Tho' you're tired and weary still journey on,
> Till you come to your happy abode
> Where all you love, you've been dreaming of
> Will be there, at the end of the road

These songs and others were sung in all the music halls and theatres during the Great War by performers and audiences trying to keep up their spirits. Men on leave from the unremitting horror of the trenches must have found the forced jollity or sentimentality difficult to understand or tolerate. The life at home must have felt a million miles away from their experiences at the front.

A visit to the Liverpool Hippodrome by war poet Siegfried Sassoon epitomises this gulf. Sassoon's disillusion with the war is clear in his poems 'Suicide in the Trenches' and 'Does it Matter?' Another war poet, Wilfred Owen, wrote the poem 'Dulce et

Decorum est Pro Patria Mori' ('It is sweet and right to die for your country') to make clear that this is not the reality of war at close quarters. Owen, whose connection with Merseyside came about when his father was appointed stationmaster at Woodside Terminus, was educated at Birkenhead School. Wilfred was 7 years old when they moved to the area. The family lived at various addresses but their last home in Higher Tranmere was 5, Milton Road. Wilfred was happy in Birkenhead and did not want to leave for Shrewsbury when his father was promoted. He had made friends and later visited Birkenhead and went to West Kirby and to Anfield. When he joined the army he encountered Liverpool soldiers and enjoyed hearing the familiar accent, so far from home. He said that it reminded him of 'Tranmere, the Pier Head, Sefton Park and such like'.

Wilfred Owen was killed in 1918, a week before the war ended.

6

COMING HOME

In Liverpool, the end of the war was announced from the Town
Hall balcony to the cheering of large crowds who had gathered to
witness the event. The Town Hall displayed the flags of the Allied
countries. The actual announcement was made by the lord mayor,
who confirmed the signing of the armistice and that firing had
ceased at eleven o'clock. There had been uncertainty about the
timing of the ceasefire but the news spread rapidly throughout the
city and many thousands of people left their places of work and
crowded into Water Street, Dale Street, Castle Street and all the
surrounding streets and alleys of central Liverpool. The bells of

Liverpool's Gun: a captured German weapon.

A photograph of Liverpool's gun—one of the German weapons captured by the British—snapshotted this afternoon. (Echo Photo)

the churches were joined by the sirens and hooters of the shipping on the River Mersey. Further along the river, the clock of Bootle Town Hall, not heard throughout the war, could now chime its familiar tones over the surrounding streets.

In the afternoon, the city was so crowded that it was difficult to move from one street to another. Wounded soldiers, soldiers on leave and groups of American soldiers were feted by the over-excited crowds. By that evening, dark though it was in November, there were many people gathered on St George's Plateau, where they sang patriotic songs. The *Liverpool Echo* reported that all the theatres and music halls were crowded and that patriotic inter-ludes were included in the programmes to the general pleasure and approval of the audiences.

Knowsley Hall, one of the ancestral homes of the Stanley family, the Earls of Derby, was prominent in service for the war effort. It had been used as a training camp, a military hospital and a convalescent home for female munitions workers, and had staged the Grand Military Gymkhana on 24 May 1915 to aid the enlistment campaign. By the end of the war, when peace was celebrated on the Derby estate with afternoon tea and sports and games, and a parade was held and naval rockets were fired, there must have been many people present whose uppermost emotion was relief that it was, apparently, all over.

And this relief, for many, would have been tempered by grief for those they had lost and anxiety for people who were not yet home, or who were wounded, even maimed for life. There would be many people whose loved ones had been posted missing, who, now, would wait in vain for them to be found and to come home. There were prisoners of war, but by far the majority of those who were missing were actually dead; with no identifiable remains, families waited with dwindling hope for news. Having survived the war, the next problem for many people, for a variety of reasons, practical and emotional, was how to survive in peacetime.

It is now recognised that soldiers who served in the Great War experienced some of the most dreadful aspects of warfare on a daily basis. The traumatic effect of the unremitting sight of the death and mutilation of their friends caused by exploding shells, machine guns or silent and deadly poison gas was reinforced by the existence of Pals battalions, where those killed or suffering were often not just their army comrades, strong though this bond might be, but also their boyhood friends or workmates.

Many thousands began suffering strange symptoms, from uncontrollable twitching or temporary paralysis to terrible nightmares. This condition became known as shell shock.

The Red Cross Military Hospital, Moss Side, in Maghull, was of particular importance in the recognition and treatment of this phenomenon, which manifested itself in a wide and bewildering range of symptoms. Moss Side became recognised internationally for research into understanding and treating shell shock. It had a specialist neurological unit from the early days of the Great War, and the first twenty patients were admitted on 7 December 1914. Initially there were 300 beds, but later this was increased to 500. This gives some insight into the scale of this problem, especially as many cases of shell shock were not being correctly diagnosed and, therefore, never reached Maghull, or anywhere else where shell shock would be sensitively treated.

Quarry Bank House, Maghull, loaned by Frank Hornby of Meccano fame.

Dr William Brown, Dr W. Rivers and Dr Elliott Smith: pioneers in treating shell shock (l–r).

There was also provision for thirty-five officers at Quarry Brook House nearby. This was the home of Frank Hornby, inventor of the Hornby 00, Meccano and Dinky cars. It was loaned for the war effort, as were many such large houses. From April 1916, it was used for severe or protracted cases only.

The pioneering work in this area done at Red Cross Military Hospital in Maghull was led by Dr Ronald Rows, who was the medical superintendent and brought together a team that had a major influence on the treatment of shell shock and on attitudes towards its sufferers. The team included Dr Elliot Smith, Dr William Brown and Dr W. Rivers. Rivers was well known for his treatment of the poet, Siegfried Sassoon, at Craiglockhart Hospital in Edinburgh.

Later in the war, other medical officers came to Maghull to attend courses at the hospital and many of them became senior figures in psychiatry, which began a process that led to a more enlightened view of mental suffering. But before this change came about there had been not only distress caused by a lack of understanding, but also in some cases a loss of honour and even life when men were accused of cowardice because of the effects of shell shock. It has been suggested that some of those who were shot for cowardice were so dazed and shattered by shell shock that they never really understood what was happening

Royal Army Medical Corps nurses in the garden at the Red Cross Hospital, Maghull.

to them. By the end of the Great War, more than 80,000 men had been diagnosed with shell shock.

Those who had fought through the war could hardly believe it when the armistice came on 11 November 1918. In most cases, the ordinary soldiers were informed by their commanding officers that the end of the fighting had arrived, although there had been some awareness that the end was in sight. Indeed, there had been a heightening of anxiety among the troops about the possibility of being killed or wounded with the end so near.

The fighting toward the end of the war was often bitter and desperate, and men were also falling prey to booby traps laid by the retreating enemy.

One of the most famous of those men killed when the war was nearly over was Wilfred Owen. He was also one of those who had been treated for shell shock. He met one of his literary heroes, Siegfried Sassoon, at the Craiglockhart War Hospital near Edinburgh where Sassoon encouraged Owen to bring his war experiences into his poetry.

Owen returned to the Western Front after more than a year away. He was awarded the Military Cross in recognition of his courage and leadership for his part in breaking the Hindenburg Line at Joncourt in October 1918. Owen was killed on 4 November 1918 during the battle to cross the Sambre-Oise Canal at Ors.

War Poets

Siegfried Sassoon and Wifred Owen were brought into contact at the shell-shock hospital at Craiglockhart. Owen, particularly, was deeply influenced by this meeting. Sassoon's courageous acts in the face of the enemy won him a Military Cross and the nickname 'Mad Jack', but his opposition to the war hardened after the Battle of the Somme in July 1916, the Battle of Arras in April 1917 and after his brother was killed. However, both Sassoon and Owen returned to the fighting.

Siegfried Sassoon (1886–1967)

Siegfried Sassoon's poem 'Blighters' was influenced by a visit to the Liverpool Hippodrome in 1917.

> The House is crammed: tier beyond tier they grin
> And cackle at the Show, while prancing ranks
> Of harlots shrill the chorus, drunk with din;
> We're sure the Kaiser loves our dear old Tanks!
> I'd like to see a Tank come down the stalls,
> Lurching to rag-time tunes, or Home, Sweet Home.
> And there'd be no more jokes in Music-halls
> To mock the riddled corpses round Bapaume.

Wilfred Owen 1893–1918

Like Siegfried Sassoon, Wilfred Owen was awarded the Military Cross. Both were brave and committed soldiers, but their verse makes it clear that they recognised the cruelty and futility of war. Owen wrote the poem 'Dulce et Decorum est', in which he called the notion that it is sweet to die for your country 'the old lie'. The phrase had often been used at the beginning of the war and is inscribed on the wall at the Royal Military Academy, Sandhurst, taken from a poem in Latin by the Roman poet, Horace. This is the first stanza:

> Bent double, like old beggars under sacks,
> Knock-kneed, coughing like hags, we cursed through sludge,
> Till on the haunting flares we turned out backs,
> And towards our distant rest began to trudge.
> Men marched asleep. Many had lost their boots,
> But limped on, blood-shod. All went lame, all blind;
> Drunk with fatigue; deaf even to the hoots
> Of gas-shells dropping softly behind.

The armistice finally came, but after the euphoria of victory was over, there were other problems to be faced. When it came to parting from old comrades, many found it difficult to say goodbye. These men had suffered unbelievably together, in loss, in fear and pain, in discomfort, loneliness and squalor. They had supported each other and had not seen their families or their homes for a long time. Now they must part to face an uncertain future without their comrades. Their families at home, however loving, could not know or imagine what these men had shared.

One of the causes of discontent and resentment was the manner in which medals were awarded. There were very few campaign medals for the Great War. Those most commonly awarded were the 1914 Star, or the 1914–1915 Star, the British War Medal and the Allied Victory Medal. These were known collectively to the men by the slightly disparaging 'Pip, Squeak and Wilfred', after a popular newspaper cartoon. The British War Medal and the Allied Victory Medal were known together as Mutt and Jeff, from the two characters in an American strip cartoon. These two medals were awarded to men who enlisted slightly later, but who may still have served for most of the war.

The medals were distributed with very little recognition of how long a man had fought or in which battles he had taken part. This meant that young lads who were only just old enough to fight at the end of the war were awarded the same medals as men who had been at the Somme or at Passchendaele. The soldiers who had been on the front line also resented the number of medals awarded to men who had been behind the lines. This might seem unimportant, but the returning soldiers needed to know that what they had endured was acknowledged by their country.

Another problem was that most of the men who lived to return home were worried about the future. How would they survive? Were their jobs still waiting for them? This was especially true for those who had been disabled. Many men would no longer be able to do the work that they had done before the war, because of various disabilities, both physical and mental. A familiar figure in Lydiate, who lived in one of three thatched

A victory parade on Lime Street, passing St George's Hall and the Empire Theatre.

cottages on Southport Road, long since demolished, was Edward Ashton. Teddy, as he was generally known, was 22 years old in 1914. He lost a leg in the Great War and, as late as the 1940s, children were fascinated by his wooden leg and the strip of old motor tyre that he nailed onto the base to avoid slipping. Teddy survived by collecting firewood from the local woodland to sell, which he balanced on one shoulder, leaving the other hand free to manage his walking stick. This form of livelihood, which depended on the support and sympathy of the community, would not have been possible in a city.

By 1922, over 1.5 million men were unemployed.

Initially, the end of the war created a boom. In Liverpool, the shipping industry expanded to take advantage of the boom, but because this was short-lived, it was followed by a slump. The war had been funded largely by borrowing, so Britain now had a large national debt. The boom in the economy had caused unemployment rates to decrease. However, when the boom was over, unemployment began to increase and men who had fought for their country found themselves out of work and unable to support their families or themselves.

A returning soldier was given a month's paid leave, still in the service of the military, after which he was officially demobilised. If he still had not found a job he was given a small unemployment benefit for about six months. After the first six months, an unemployed ex-soldier would have to join the dole queue.

Unemployed former soldiers found themselves unwanted. They suffered loss of self-respect and anxiety about their survival and their ability to support a family, and they began to feel bitter about the apparent ingratitude of the nation.

The government, under prime minister David Lloyd George, needed to act quickly as more men were sent home who could not find jobs. The Unemployment Insurance Act of 1920 changed the laws of 1911, raising the amount of dole money given and the number of workers who could claim.

One of the consequences of concerns about jobs for the returning men was the effect this had on the employment of women.

It may be that, at the beginning of their wartime employment, women had understood that this was a temporary situation – that it was, in fact, seen as their war service to replace a man who was needed at the front. However, more than four years is a long period of time and some women resented being dismissed to make way for the returning forces. A woman's desire to remain in work was sometimes caused by the fact that her husband was a returning soldier who had not yet found employment. What she could earn was crucial to meet the needs of the family, although she might have been glad to return to the home if there had been work for men.

Long years of anxiety for their menfolk had added to the pressures of wartime employment, which in some cases were a heavy burden that women were glad to relinquish. Employed women had still been obliged to perform housework, cook and perhaps care for children or elderly relatives. These pressures made the withdrawal of many women back into their homes after the war less surprising. But the willingness to return to full-time domesticity was not wholly voluntary or wholesale.

There were changes that made it impossible for some women to continue to work outside their homes. Some jobs had become available to women during wartime, but when hostilities ceased, these opportunities disappeared. Servicemen expected, justifiably, to return to the jobs they had left. Attitudes to what was suitable work for women had not changed entirely and it was expected that women who had taken on heavy jobs, such as tram drivers, or dirty jobs, such as train cleaners, would be glad to relinquish them.

There were many women who remained unmarried after the war and there was a widespread suggestion in the press that the huge numbers of casualties and permanently disabled amounted to a 'lost generation' of young men. During the following decade, single women were sometimes referred to as 'surplus' women, implying that there was no purpose for their existence beyond marriage and motherhood.

In fact, the situation was more complex than this suggests. It was mostly middle-class women who remained single, partly because the relatively narrow social group of men who could be seen as acceptable husbands had largely been of the officer class, and this social group had been cruelly reduced because of the tradition of 'leading from the front'. The middle and upper classes were reduced disproportionately by the war because it was these social groups who provided the junior officers whose job it was to lead their men over the top and expose themselves to the greatest danger.

About 12 per cent of ordinary soldiers were killed during the war, while 17 per cent of officers were killed. Eton alone lost more than 1,000 former pupils, which was 20 per cent of those old boys who served. This was mirrored in other public schools. The prime minister at the beginning of the war, Herbert Asquith, lost a son, and a future prime minister, Andrew Bonar Law, lost two sons. Anthony Eden lost two brothers; another brother of his was terribly wounded and an uncle was a prisoner of war.

Alongside the reduced opportunities for marriage, there were women who remained single by choice.

The Sex Disqualification (Removal) Act of 1919 made it illegal to exclude women from jobs because of their gender. So, educated middle-class women found that some of the professions were suddenly more accessible, in theory. These professions, such as medicine and teaching, were beginning to open up to women but only if they were unmarried.

In some occupations, single women insisted on excluding their married sisters. For instance, in 1921, female civil servants passed a resolution asking for the banning of married women from their jobs. The resulting ban was enforced until 1946.

During the war, hospitals had accepted female medical students, but in the 1920s, women were rejected by the hospitals on the grounds of modesty.

The National Association of Schoolmasters campaigned against the employment of female teachers. In 1924, the London County Council make its policy explicit when it changed the phrase 'shall resign on marriage' to 'the contract shall end on marriage'. Presumably, it was concerned that some women might refuse to resign. The situation elsewhere varied with the need for teachers.

Women were also divided among themselves on this issue, with single and widowed women claiming a prior right to employment over married women. A letter from a woman to the *Daily Herald* in 1919 declared, 'No decent man would allow his wife to work, and no decent woman would do it if she knew the harm she was doing to the widows and single girls who are looking for work.' It continued, 'Put the married women out, send them home to clean their houses and look after the man they married and give a mother's care to their children. Give the single women and widows the work.' This view was particularly endorsed by the general public when the widows involved were war widows.

The effect of losing their jobs, and the response to this loss, must have varied greatly between women. Married women whose husbands had returned safely, and particularly those whose husbands had returned to gainful employment, would have been far less resentful than women whose husbands had been killed or seriously injured, or whose future employment was uncertain. In all these cases, women would have become the main breadwinners. They may have had children to support as well as a disabled husband. Yet they knew that, in effect, they were seen by some of these letter-writers and campaigners as married women who should not be part of the workforce.

Contracts of employment during the war had usually been based on collective agreements between trade unions and employers, which decided that women would only be employed 'for the duration of the war'. Some employed mothers were hit by the closure of day nurseries that had been vastly extended during the war. The general view was that these arrangements would no longer be needed, but, for widows and women with disabled husbands, the need for wages and childcare was vital.

Reinforcing these pressures were the recriminatory voices of returning servicemen. As unemployment levels soared immediately after the war, anger towards women 'taking' jobs from men built up.

The Women's Social and Political Union (WSPU) had suspended campaigning for women's suffrage during the war. The movement had recognised their obligation to support the war effort, but also realised that such support could be of benefit to them in the end.

In some countries, women's war service was recognised by the right to vote. Politicians and people in general believed that women deserved greater political rights. The Representation of the People Act, February 1918, gave the vote to all men over 21 years of age and to women over 30 years who met minimum property qualifications or were married to men who owned such property. In December 1919, Lady Astor became the first woman to take a seat in Parliament. But it was not until the Equal Franchise Act of 1928 that women were allowed to vote from the age of 21.

So the women who benefited in 1918 were over 30 years of age and, in some cases, married. Many younger women who had worked so hard in munitions and other factories, on the buses, delivering the post, and in very many other occupations were given no recognition by the government.

It is clear that the pre-war women's movements had prepared the way for this change. For instance, in France, where there had been no women's suffrage movement before the war, women were not enfranchised despite their war efforts. It seems likely that politicians feared the resumption of protest if no concessions were made to women's rights and believed that the country needed a period of stability in order to recover from the trauma of war. It is clear that the extension of the franchise to some women was not a recognition that women were men's equals.

From early in the Great War, it became clear that existing government departments did not have the facilities, organisation or resources to deal with discharged and disabled men. After the outbreak of war on 4 August 1914, the British Red Cross formed a Joint War Committee with the Order of St John. The two organisations worked together and combined their fundraising activities and resources. One of their concerns was to help wounded soldiers to rehabilitate in hospital during and after the war; previously almost no provision had been made for their treatment or rehabilitation. This was not a new problem; it was centuries old. After many earlier wars, disbanded soldiers had been a problem, but the sheer weight of numbers and the recruitment of thousands of non-professionals into the services made it impossible to ignore after the First World War.

The Red Cross established homes with workshops where men could learn a trade, such as carpentry, boot-making, basketwork or woodwork. Every effort was made to find work for those who recovered sufficiently and about three-quarters of the men were found employment.

In 1916, Queen Mary expressed concern for the long-term future of servicemen injured in the war, and she was given possession of the Star and Garter Hotel in Richmond, Surrey. The queen requested that the Red Cross should convert the hotel into a 'permanent haven' for disabled ex-servicemen.

There was sufficient space for 180 patients and over 60 members of staff. There were workshops, a gym and a cinema, and the residents took part in social events and activities, as well as training and treatment. They became skilled craftsmen, who produced good-quality items for sale.

It had taken in the first residents on 14 January 1916; its original purpose was to care for severely disabled young men returning from the battlefields. But its work was far from completed when hostilities ceased. Later, several other homes were opened, including one in Southport. The Royal Star & Garter Homes remains a charity that continues to provide outstanding nursing and therapeutic care to the ex-service community.

An annual exhibition and sale of work began in 1924 and was visited by distinguished guests including the Duchess of York, who had married into the royal family in 1923. Elizabeth Bowes-Lyon, daughter of the Earl of Strathmore and Kinghorne, became queen in 1936, following the abdication of her brother-in-law, and was later to become Queen Elizabeth, the Queen Mother.

Postscript: Legacy

When the war ended, after a natural period of jubilation, people awoke to the bleak fact that time was not going to turn back to before the war began, simply because the war had ended. Thousands had been killed; they were not going to come home, and each one was mourned again by a whole family, street or community. Others had a family member who had gone away as a boy in a spirit of adventure and now returned to them, old before their time, sometimes maimed in body or in spirit.

No one was untouched.

William Ratcliffe MM, VC, described as 'the dockers' VC', came home to a hero's welcome. The *Liverpool Echo* reported that the pavement in Brindley Street, Toxteth Park, where Bill had lived with his married sister, had been scrubbed from end to end and every house sported a flag, streamers or bunting. When he arrived home, all the people from the district came out to greet him and the local school, St Vincent de Paul RC Primary School, Norfolk Street, off Park Lane, which he had attended, gave a hero's reception for him. Bill earned his medals at Messines in 1917, and was decorated by the king at Buckingham Palace soon after.

What sort of world did he return to after the war?

Everyone from the highest to the lowest had been touched, and in most cases damaged, by the war. Every social class was affected. During the war more than 200 generals had been killed, wounded or captured. They had not all been as remote from the

'King' William the Conqueror

"I WAS SO pleased when I read your column (February 16) and also very grateful to Mr Lindsay," writes Mrs N. Dwyer, of West Derby.

"Among Mr Lindsay's list of VCs was William Ratcliffe and I recall the homecoming of this brave soldier 74 years ago.

"I think that he lived in Brindley Street, off Jamaica Street.

"Everyone from the surrounding streets gathered there to welcome him.

"As a little girl, with my mother, I remember the cheers and clapping when he arrived in a horse-drawn carriage which, I suppose, was the Lord Mayor's coach.

"I attended St Vincent's School, Norfolk Street, off Park Lane.

"It was a great honour for the school as William Ratcliffe had been a pupil there

and a celebration was planned for him.

"A raised platform was built in the playground and all the local dignitaries, our clergy and teachers were present.

"The pupils were assembled amd we sang this song:

Billy, Billy Ratcliffe, you are a great brave-hearted man,
A credit to your country and all your native land.
May your arm be ever steady and your aim be ever true,
God bless you, Billy Ratcliffe, here is your country's love to you.

"To all the brave men of yesteryear, and the brave men of the present, now serving in the Gulf, God bless you. Here's your country's love to you!" adds Mrs Dwyer.

FOOTNOTE: Private Ratcliffe (who also won the Military Medal) was awarded the VC for locating an enemy machine-gun firing at his comrades from the rear. Single-handed, he rushed the post, bayoneted all its crew and returned to his own lines with the gun. He died in 1963.

August, 1917, and Private William Ratcliffe, VC, shakes hands with King George V. An ex-Liverpool docker, Bill, who latterly lived at 29A St OswaldGardens, Old Swan, was known as "The dockers' VC".

William Ratcliffe MM, VC remembered in the Liverpool Echo, 1991.

action or protected from harm as has sometimes been portrayed. The strict social hierarchy of an earlier England, accepted for centuries without question, had disappeared, partly because of the disproportionately high percentage of casualties among the landed classes. Ancient families had lost their heirs or faced crippling death duties, and their estates were broken up, becoming schools, golf clubs and hotels.

Visitors to National Trust properties will be aware that a number of large houses and estates came to the Trust because there was no surviving heir or because multiple death duties had made it impossible for the estates to go on as they had done for so long. Many of the men and women who had been in the servant class were not willing to return to that life, so the great estates could not be so easily staffed and managed.

So instead of these estates existing exclusively for the privileged few, while providing employment for many, they became places of historical interest, leisure or education, where all social classes could wander at will.

Society had changed in ways that meant nothing would ever be the same. It was less stratified. Ordinary people were much more inclined to question the rights of those who were richer or socially elevated to order the lives of everyone else. It was also difficult to find domestic staff for smaller homes. These had been largely staffed by one or two girls who did all the work of the home and earned very little. Now they had found other ways to earn a living, which allowed them greater freedom. Manufacturers, in the 1920s, began to market labour-saving devices to enable women who had never cleaned their own houses to do so. There was no going back, since these advances made it easier for married women to consider working outside the home.

At the end of the war, in November 1918, there were nearly 4 million men in the British Army. In twelve months' time, this had been reduced to 900,000. But demobilisation was not without its problems. The war secretary, Lord Derby, suggested that the men who should be released first were those who had held posts in important branches of industry. This made sense in terms of efficiency for the nation, but not in terms of common justice. Many of those who would have been demobbed first were those with the least service.

When Winston Churchill became war secretary in January 1919, he introduced a new system of demobilisation, which was much more just. Churchill's system was based on age, length of service and the number of times a man had been wounded in the fighting. This was accepted as fair by the servicemen and avoided further tensions.

More than 750,000 British men died during the First World War. This was 9 per cent of all British men under the age of 45. In the ranks of ordinary soldiers, about 12 per cent had been killed. Those who were left believed that they had fought not just against the enemy, but also for the right to a better life. The survivors were less deferential than people had customarily been before 1914. Officers had been obliged to earn the respect of their men in the trenches. Moreover, years of obeying orders to the point of death meant that men were not willing to 'tug their forelocks' in civilian life. They had been promised 'a land fit for heroes'. Ordinary men and women were demanding improvements in housing, steady employment and education for their children.

A legacy of the period after the war was the high number of council houses that were built. Before the war, new housing was built privately and could not be afforded by many who had fought. But servicemen did not want to come home to slum housing. They had been promised 'homes for heroes'.

The Housing and Town Planning Act of 1919 (The Addison Act) allowed corporations to provide housing. These were usually three-bedroom houses on modest-sized estates. The houses usually had a decent-sized garden, so that tenants would grow their own food and, therefore, improve on the pre-war diet and health of the lower social classes. Schools and shops were provided and, sometimes, churches were built, often a daughter church to an already existing ancient parish church, such as St Aidan's church in Cherry Lane, Walton, attached to the oldest church in the West Derby Hundred, St Mary's, Walton-on-the Hill.

All the houses had a scullery, a bath and a flush toilet. These conditions were a vast improvement on the overcrowding and lack of basic facilities previously endured by many families. Such estates were built, for instance, in Walton, West Derby, Woolton and Fazakerley. Most had tree-lined roads and front gardens with privet hedges. There was also provision for allotment gardens so that people could grow fresh produce to feed their families. One corporation estate in Walton had such allotments in Atheldene Road. The Liverpool corporation houses were well maintained and much sought after for many years. People were proud to live in them.

The need to increase industrial efficiency for the war effort meant that the working class had become more powerful and much better organised during the war, so they were by no means as powerless as they had been in the past. Most of those returning from the war were reintegrated successfully. Although in Germany discontented ex-servicemen were radicalised politically, in Britain ex-servicemen tended to group themselves around the forerunners of the local branches of the British Legion.

The British Legion was formed on 15 May 1921, bringing together four national organisations of ex-servicemen that had established themselves after the First World War.

The original intention of the British Legion had been to help those who were suffering because of service to their country, either those who were limited in their capacity to earn a living by injury or mental hurt, or war widows and their children. The work goes on: £321,000 was recently raised by the sale of a special edition of Liverpool FC shirts. These were embroidered with poppies – that iconic symbol of the battlefields – and had been worn by Liverpool players in their match against Chelsea on Remembrance Sunday.

Toc H was also formed as a consequence of the Great War. The army chaplain, the Reverend Phillip Thomas Byard (Tubby) Clayton, was sent to France and, afterwards, to Poperinge in Belgium. This was a busy transfer station where troops on their way to and from the battlefields of Flanders were billeted. Tubby was asked by the senior chaplain, Neville Talbot, to set up some sort of rest house for the troops.

Tubby set up Talbot House in honour of Gilbert Talbot, Neville's brother, who had been killed earlier that year. It was not conventionally a 'church' house, more an open house for the men. Talbot House soon became known by its initials TH, and then, in the radio signallers' usage, as Toc H. It opened on 11 December 1915. Toc H has survived and evolved to become an international Christian movement for good.

The war had brought about changes, both political and social. Some change was gradual in practice. For instance, although some women had gained the right to vote in 1918, there were only eight women Members of Parliament in 1923 and women over the age of 21 were not able to vote until 1928.

The changes in women's attitudes were more apparent in their appearance. Women who had served in the auxiliary services or worked in manufacturing, transport and on the land had necessarily adapted their dress. They had worn a range of uniforms and practical clothing, even trousers when these were appropriate to their activities. This change to more practical clothing during wartime accelerated the pace of change afterwards. Women did not want to return to restrictive and uncomfortable clothing. They began to wear shorter skirts and short hairstyles. Manners were more relaxed and some women began to smoke in public, although this was considered 'fast' and was not generally accepted.

Some of the changes after the war appeared trivial, but were symbolic of public feeling about the Germans. People did not want dogs that they thought were German, so German Shepherd dogs became known as 'Alsatians' in 1919. The name of German Shepherd dogs was not reinstated by the English Kennel Club until 1977.

After the war, people wanted to create worthy memorials to the fallen. They wanted to respect their sacrifice and make sure that future generations understood both the enormous numbers of the country's loss and, at the same time, the importance of each individual sacrifice.

THE HOUSE OF WINDSOR
At the beginning of the war, the royal house was Saxe-Coburg Gotha, Queen Victoria's name on marriage to the German, Prince Albert. In 1917, George V accepted his secretary, Lord Stamfordham's suggestion that Windsor, symbolic of the ancient castle, enduring and steeped in English history, would be a better choice.

The Cenotaph in Whitehall, London, designed by Sir Edwin Lutyens, became the focus for the nation's public acts of remembrance. In cities, towns and villages throughout the nation, memorials sprang up. The money for them was raised by public subscription, with donations both large and small.

There were large and imposing memorials, like the Cenotaph on St George's Plateau in Liverpool designed by well-known architects and artists. It is a rectangular stone edifice with bronze,

The Liverpool Cenotaph, St George's Plateau.

147

A detail of servicemen on the Cenotaph, where so many last saw Liverpool.

low-relief sculptures of servicemen and mourners. It was designed by Lionel Budden and carved by Herbert Tyson Smith.

There are 1,046 Great War memorials listed on the Merseyside Roll of Honour website. These include churches of all denominations, schools, boys' clubs and sports clubs, Bible classes, football clubs, the University of Liverpool, post offices, banks, the police, the fire brigade, shipping lines, the tramways and many others. They vary from a simple plaque to the memorial in Maghull, which is the Church of England school building itself.

People still have a high regard for war memorials. In Ormskirk, the post office on Aughton Street closed in 2017; the memorial plaque has been removed to the Ormskirk sorting office, with a service of rededication.

In Westminster Abbey, the Tomb of the Unknown Warrior provided a poignant focus for the grief of all those people whose loved ones had 'no known grave'. Chosen through a careful

POST OFFICE MEMORIALS

One of the numerous post office memorials was originally in the main hall of the Post Office, Whitechapel, Liverpool, then in the General Post Office in Victoria Street, but is now situated in the Metquarter, Victoria Street. It was originally unveiled on 15 June 1924, and rededicated on 8 March 2006.

process to ensure anonymity, the warrior was interred with ceremony 'amongst the Kings'.

As no one could know the identity of the young man, he could have been anyone's lost child, husband, father or brother; the new Duchess of York placed her bouquet on the tomb as she left the abbey on her wedding day in 1923. At the time of her wedding, the body of her brother, Fergus, an officer in the Black Watch who was killed during the Battle of Loos, had not been found.

A stained-glass window in the Chapter House of Liverpool's Anglican Cathedral bears the legend 'In memory of the Freemasons of the Province who for the love of their fellows and in the cause of justice gave their lives in the Great War.'

In 2017, a memorial commemorating sixty-four Freemason VCs was unveiled. Arthur Herbert Procter's name appears upon it.

Arthur Procter 1890–1973 was born in Church Street, Bootle. He joined the VAD in August 1914, but by November he had enlisted in the King's (Liverpool) Regiment. In June 1916, at Ficheau, south of Arras, Arthur went into no-man's land under heavy fire to succour two injured men. He dressed their wounds and dragged them to the shelter of a bank. Both men were brought out alive at dusk. He received the Victoria Cross from King George V, in the presence of Sir Douglas Haig and General Joffre.

In August 1916, Arthur was granted leave and was officially received at his battalion headquarters by the lord mayor of Liverpool. From there he was carried shoulder-high to Liverpool Produce Exchange, where he was presented with a gold watch, a cheque for 100 guineas and a £100 4½ per cent War Loan.

Arthur left his work in the provisions trade; he was ordained in 1927 and served as a chaplain to the Royal Air Force from 1941 to 1946. After many years as a vicar, Arthur retired in 1965.

In Lydiate, children from St Thomas Church of England Primary School and St Gregory's Catholic Primary School joined together in 2016 in a series of events and activities funded by the Heritage Lottery to remember the twenty-four Lydiate men who fell. Their names are commemorated on lecterns in the gardens of the two schools and include Herbert Finch, who lived on the boundary of Lydiate and Maghull and, perhaps because of this, was missed from the memorials in both villages. In, 2017, the children of Lydiate Primary School also followed a series of talks and activities and an act of remembrance.

As well as public war memorials, great and small, collective and individual, many homes throughout the land contained smaller items of significance.

Sadly, many homes had, often framed and hanging on the wall near to a photograph of the lost family member, the Memorial Plaque issued to the next-of-kin of all British and Empire service personnel who had been killed. This bronze plaque, about 5in across and very heavy, came to be known as 'the Dead Man's Penny' because it bore a resemblance to the smaller penny coin.

Lydiate schoolchildren unveil their First World War Memory Board in their Peace Garden.

Another small artefact treasured by many families is Princess Mary's 1914 Christmas Gift. This is an embossed brass box that originally contained a variety of items such as tobacco and chocolate. It was intended as a Christmas present to 'every sailor afloat and every soldier at the front' in 1914 and it was paid for

*Princess Mary's
1914 Christmas Gift
to my grandfather.*

by a public fund backed by Princess Mary. Eventually it was given to all who were serving, to prisoners of war and the next of kin of 1914 casualties. It is estimated that about 2,620,019 gifts were given, but although they are not rare, they are valued.

The smokers' and non-smokers' gifts were considered to be unsuitable for nurses at the front in France who were given the box, a packet of chocolate and the card instead. The embossed brass box was airtight, and was, therefore, a useful container for money, tobacco, papers and photographs, especially in the appalling conditions of trench warfare. So the boxes were often carried through the whole of the war.

A great many men carefully repacked their presents and sent them home to their wives and families, which is what was done by my grandfather. I have the box given to my grandfather, Albert Sendall of Allendale Avenue, Aintree, who was serving in the Mercantile Marine – if he had not sent it home, it would almost certainly have been lost at sea on one of the two occasions when his ships were torpedoed.

In 2014, the Bishop of Liverpool, the Right Rev. Paul Bayes, led services at Walton church and the Alsop High School to remember the young

THE WALTON PALS

Thirty of the young men who were members of the Young Men's Bible Class at Walton church and joined the King's (Liverpool) Regiment were killed at the Somme. They are remembered at the Thiepval Memorial and in Walton church: there a small silver chalice is inscribed with one of their names, Percy Tucker, and on a brass lectern all thirty names are inscribed.

The Mercantile Marine War Medal, established 1919.

men from Walton who gave their lives during the Battle of the Somme. Joe Mangan, Alsop's head teacher, said that the school 'felt it was important to commemorate the young men from our community who fell at the Battle of the Somme'.

Across the city and the region of Liverpool, people of all ages have joined together on many occasions to remember the events and sacrifices of a century ago and to make a reality of the words, 'We will remember them.'

'The Weeping Window': Liverpool poppies at St George's Hall.

Bibliography and Further Reading

Books

Arthur, Max, *Last Post* (Phoenix, 2005)

Bailey, F.A., and Millington, R., *The Story of Liverpool* (Merseyside Press, 1957)

Benbough-Jackson, Mike, *Merseyside's War* (Amberley Publishing, 2015)

Braybon, Gail, *Women Workers in the First World War* (Croom Helm, 1981)

Davies, Lesley, and Ewing, Dave, *Sefton At War* (Sefton Council, 2014)

Gilbert, Martin, *Somme: The Heroism and Horror of War* (John Murray, 2006)

Harrop, Sylvia, *The Merchant Taylors' School for Girls* (Liverpool University Press, 1988)

Hildrey, Trevor W., *To Answer Duty's Call* (Osprey Publishing, 2015)

Knowsley Hall: a guide book for visitors. 1955. Liverpool Record Office, Liverpool 942.7213

Macdonald, Lyn, *The Roses of No Man's Land* (Penguin, 1980)

McGreal, Stephen, *Liverpool in the Great War* (Pen and Sword Military, 2014)

Paxman, Jeremy, *Great Britain's Great War* (Viking, 2013)

Records of Edmund Kirby & Sons 1916–19. Liverpool Record
Office, Liverpool 720 KIR/1429

Rothwell, Catherine, *Liverpool in Old Photographs* (Budding Books,
1996)

Rowlands, John K. *Around Maghull and Lydiate* (The Chalford
Publishing Company, 1997)

Russell, Pamela, 'Liverpool's Past: A Magical History Tour', in
A. Grant and C. Grey (eds), *The Mersey Sound* (Open House
Press, 2007)

Russell, Pamela, *Lydiate's Great War 1914–1918* (Heritage Lottery
Fund, 2016)

Smith, Angela K., *Women's Writing of the First World War*
(Manchester University Press, 2000)

The Silver Jubilee Book (Odhams Press Ltd, 1935)

Twist, Colin, *A History of the Liverpool Parks* (Hobby Publications,
2000)

Williams, P.H., *Liverpolitana* (Merseyside Civic Society, 1971)

Websites

www.theliverpoolpalsmemorialfund.com/history.php

www.bbc.co.uk

www.cwgc.org

www.merseyside-at-war.org

www.merseysiderollofhonour.co.uk

www.ancestry.co.uk

www.liverpoolecho.co.uk

www.iwm.org.uk

www.victoriacross.org.uk

Great War Britain:
The First World War at Home

Luci Gosling

After the declaration of war in 1914, the conflict dominated civilian life for the next four years. Magazines quickly adapted without losing their gossipy essence: fashion jostled for position with items on patriotic fundraising, and court presentations were replaced by notes on nursing. The result is a fascinating, amusing and uniquely feminine perspective of life on the home front.

978 0 7524 9188 2

The Workers' War:
British Industry and the First World War

Anthony Burton

The First World War didn't just rock the nation in terms of bloodshed: it was a war of technological and industrial advances. Working Britain experienced change as well: with the men at war, it fell to the women of the country to keep the factories going. Anthony Burton explores that change.

978 0 7524 9886 7

Visit our website and discover many other First World War books.

www.thehistorypress.co.uk/first-world-war